NEEDLEPOINT
C•A•T•S

Julie Hasler

David & Charles

This book is dedicated to Leannda Cross, my co-designer, another cat fanatic. Thank you so much, Leannda, for all your hard work and dedication. I hope that one day you achieve all of your ambitions and goals as an artist, and find true happiness.

A DAVID & CHARLES BOOK

First published in the UK in 1998

A catalogue record for this book is available from the British Library.

ISBN 0 7153 0393 7

Photography by Di Lewis
Book design by Jane Forster

printed in Italy
by Lego SpA

for David & Charles
Brunel House   Newton Abbot   Devon

CONTENTS

THE PROJECTS

INTRODUCTION

Being recognised mainly for my feline portrayals, I am often asked, 'Why cats?' The answer is that I create cat designs simply because I absolutely love cats! I love everything about them and feel totally in tune with them. As an artist, I find their grace and beauty, and their every move a constant source of inspiration. Everyone who has cats will know that each one has its own individual personality, and on no account must they be underestimated. They are glorious creatures and make ideal companions as they are clean, intelligent, friendly and affectionate.

There have been cats in my family for as long as I can remember. My parents got me my first kitten at the age of five whilst returning from a holiday in Kent. We had stopped off at a farm to buy a sack of potatoes and on approaching the farmhouse, we heard the sound of mewing coming from a nearby barn. There we saw a row of tiny kittens' heads peering from beneath the barn door. They were so sweet that my mother asked the farmer if we could see them. He showed us into the barn, and told us that the mother cat was a stray who had come into the barn to give birth to her kittens. Although they had been feeding the mother while she was caring for her kittens, he told us that they had to get rid of them soon, as they were causing a nuisance. Being very concerned about this, my mother told me to choose one to take home. I picked the prettiest one of the litter, a female long-haired tortoiseshell that we later named Puskin. This began my lifelong passion for cats.

Even as a child I was a keen artist and used to spend hours drawing and painting, finding cats ideal subjects. As I got older I became interested in photography, and would visit animal shelters with my camera, taking photographs of the cats and later using these as sources for my drawing and painting. When I became interested in needlepoint and cross stitch, it was my frustration at not being able to find designs of cats on the market that I liked, that inspired me to start designing my own charts, eventually getting the first one published in a craft magazine at the age of eighteen, and my first contract for a book of cat designs at the age of twenty-one.

I have shared my life with many cats as I am unable to ignore their suffering – at one time I had eleven. If I see a stray, or hear of an unwanted or neglected cat, I just have to have it. I only have three now – Kym, a Burmese who came from Wood Green animal shelter, and Ben and Garfie who are half Persian litter mates that I fell in love with in a pet shop while buying some food for my dogs!

Having these cats seemed to trigger off some sort of obsession within me. I buy cat related items wherever I go, consequently my house is full of cat things. Framed prints, water-colours, and embroideries adorn the walls, there are cat cushions, ornaments, jewellery, bathroom accessories and even a cat lamp!

While researching ideas for this book, I was lucky enough to meet Leannda Cross, a young artist who had just left art school and was as crazy as me about cats. Being able to work in many mediums and having the ability and flexibility to work in many different styles, we made an ideal partnership. I already knew exactly what I wanted in the book and how I wanted it presented, which breeds I wanted to feature on which backgrounds and what the finished embroideries would be made into. Leannda was totally in tune with me on this and after much research into the different breeds and their origins, we began choosing the background designs.

Everything had to be correct and authentic. For example, the patchwork designs in the set of four Patchwork-Style Cushions are true patchwork designs, not just stylized images of patchwork shapes. In the rectangular Sleepy Cat Cushions, the breed of cat is featured on a background relating to its origin; thus the British Tabby is on a William Morris inspired background, the Persian is on a background inspired by an authentic Persian rug, and so on. Leannda and I worked very closely in the initial stages to make sure

Above: *The four Sleepy Cat Cusions (see pages 62–75)*
Right: *Zoe's Favourite Toy (see page 118)*

we totally understood each others ideas and aims, and after many months of hard work, Leannda produced the beautiful paintings from which the charts in the book were created.

Needlepoint Cats is for all those who have known and have loved the cat. An intriguing treasury of fascinating felines, characterisation of cat breeds, beautiful designs exquisitely presented and illustrated throughout, this book will be a joy to give or to receive and certainly to cherish forever.

MATERIALS AND EQUIPMENT

Needlepoint is worked with wool or thread over canvas and the stitches cover the whole area, including the background. This means that the finished embroidery is strong, heavy and very durable, making it particularly suitable for upholstery and soft furnishings, such as footstools, cushion covers, chair seats, rugs and decorative wall hangings. It is also ideal for small, practical items like spectacle cases and purses.

One of the great attractions of needlepoint is that beautiful and useful objects can be created with the minimum of materials and equipment. Canvas, needles, threads and a tapestry frame are all that are really required.

CANVAS
Canvas produced specifically for needlepoint is constructed from an even mesh of horizontal and vertical threads. As well as canvas made from cotton, which has been used to create the projects in this book, canvas is available in linen, silk and plastic. Plastic canvas is a particularly good medium for children to learn needlepoint on, as the holes are large and easier to work, and mistakes can easily be cut out or unpicked without damaging the canvas.

There are two types of canvas in general use: one is woven with single threads (mono canvas), and the other with double threads (duo canvas), which has pairs of threads running vertically and horizontally. The projects in this book are worked on both single- and double-thread canvas. Canvas is graded by the mesh size, which is the number of stitches it gives to the inch (2.5cm), also referred to as the 'count'. Thus 10 count canvas has 10 holes to the inch (2.5cm). This can be gauged by counting the number of holes to the inch (2.5cm). The finer the canvas, the more holes there are to the inch. The designs in this book are worked on various mesh sizes. If you wish to alter the size of the finished embroidery, choose a canvas which

has more (or less) holes to the inch, and the finished design will be smaller (or larger) accordingly.

Always ensure that you buy good quality canvas, such as Zweigart. Cheaper versions may be of inferior quality and have broken threads, knots or an uneven weave which will distort the finished design.

THREADS
The needlepoint projects in this book are worked in DMC threads. The projects worked on 10 count canvas are worked in DMC tapestry wool, which is a superior quality non-divisible 4-ply wool which is both mothproof and colourfast. Projects worked on the finer mesh canvas are worked in DMC six-strand stranded cottons. Both threads are available in 8m (8¾yd) skeins, and in over 400 colours and shades, enabling you to achieve subtle blendings and delicate shaded effects.

The exact amount of strands used with a particular canvas will be determined by the individual, as people tend to work at different tensions, which effects the coverage of the canvas. DMC recommend the following amount of strands of embroidery cotton are used on the mono canvas:

10 count, use 9–12 strands
14 count, use 6–9 strands
18 count, use 3 strands
20 count, use 2 strands
22 count, use 2 strands.

Gold and silver thread has also been included in some of the projects and details of this can be found with the specific project.

NEEDLES
Needlepoint is worked with tapestry needles which have a blunt point. They are available in various

numbered sizes to suit the canvas mesh size being worked on. The finer the needle, the higher its number. The needle should pass through the canvas easily without pushing the threads apart and the eye should be held in place by the canvas threads without allowing the needle to fall through. For example, use a No.18 tapestry needle on 10 mesh duo canvas, and a No.24 on 14 mesh mono canvas. The size of needle required for each design is given with the project.

As most needles are made of steel, they tend to tarnish or rust with age. Therefore, do not leave your needle in the design area when you are not working on the embroidery, as it can leave unsightly marks on the canvas or thread. If you find that your needle does become tarnished, or rough to the touch through use, it is best to discard it, as it may catch and damage the canvas and thread.

You may think it worth the investment to buy gold-plated or even platinum needles which are now available in many needlework shops. They are a pleasure to use, as they slide through the canvas with less friction and will not rust or mark the canvas.

TAPESTRY FRAMES

It is advisable to work needlepoint on a rotating wooden frame, either a floor-standing model for larger projects, or a hand-held frame for smaller ones. Both are available in several sizes. The frame consists of two horizontal rollers with tapes onto which the canvas is sewn. These rollers slot into two vertical stretchers and are held in place by screws and wing-nuts. The canvas is rolled onto the rollers until it is taut, and then is laced to the stretchers. The frame holds the canvas at a permanent tension: this makes it easier to work, keeps the stitching even and helps to maintain the shape of the canvas until the needlepoint is finished. When buying a frame, pay particular attention to the smoothness of the wood from which it is made, and the free running of the rollers. Do not use an embroidery hoop, as they are unsuitable for canvas work.

If you have not worked on a frame before, practice by working a few rows of stitches at the edge of the canvas, to get used to using the frame before starting a design. You will find that you are able to push the needle up through the canvas with one hand and down with the other.

Although some of the designs in this book are small enough to work without a tapestry frame, I would not personally recommend working needle-point 'in the hand' (without a frame), unless you are an experienced stitcher and are able to work the design without it becoming distorted. If you do decide to work in the hand, you may find that the raw edges of the canvas damage the thread as you sew, and also snag your clothing. To avoid this happening, bind the rough edges of the canvas with masking tape.

SCISSORS

You will need two pairs of sharp scissors: a medium-sized pair of dress-making scissors for cutting and trimming canvas and backing fabrics, and a small pair of pointed embroidery scissors for cutting threads is essential, especially if a mistake has to be rectified. Look after your scissors and they will serve you well. Keep them clean, try not to drop them and do not use either pair for cutting paper or you will find that they will blunt very quickly.

BASIC TECHNIQUES

PREPARATION

Ensure that you work in good light. Daylight is preferable but not always possible so daylight simulation bulbs are a good option. Specialist magnifiers and magnifier lamps are also available from many needlework shops and are a great help when working on fine canvas.

Ensure that you work in a comfortable position and while stitching keep your hands and working area clean, as light-coloured threads will show up any dirt, and darker threads will show up any pet hairs or fluff from jumpers.

POSITIONING THE DESIGN

Where you make your first stitch is important as this will determine the position of the finished design on your canvas. First, you will need to find the exact centre point of the chart by counting along one hor-

izontal edge and then one vertical edge to find the middle grid line of each, then follow these to their intersection. Next, locate the centre of your canvas by folding it in half vertically and then horizontally, pinching along the folds. Mark along these lines with tacking stitches or a fabric marker if you prefer. The centre stitch of your design will lie where the folds in the canvas meet. Where you begin to stitch is entirely up to you. Some people prefer to start with a particular motif or colour at the central point and work outwards to the edges; others prefer to start at the top and work down. Personally, I recommend the latter. To locate the top, count the squares up from the centre of the chart, and then count left to the first symbol. Next, count the corresponding number of holes up and across from the centre of the canvas and begin at that point. Remember that each square on the chart represents one stitch on the canvas.

MOUNTING CANVAS IN A TAPESTRY FRAME

If using a rotating frame, the canvas first needs to be attached to the tape or webbing at the top and bottom horizontal rollers of the frame. Starting from the centre of the webbing, hem stitch the canvas in place. The canvas is then rolled around the bars, at the top or bottom (depending on the area of canvas being worked) until it is taut. The wing-nuts are tightened and the canvas is then laced to the side stretchers.

FOLLOWING A CHART

The designs are shown in coloured chart form: each square on the chart represents one needlepoint stitch to be taken on the canvas. The symbol in the square denotes the thread colour to be used, and corresponds to the colour key listed with each chart. This gives a colour description for each symbol, plus the DMC shade number.

You may find it easier to enlarge the chart you intend to stitch from using a photocopier, so that the squares and colours are easier to see.

STITCHING TECHNIQUES

There are many different needlepoint stitches, some more detailed and decorative than others; this book, however, concentrates on tent stitch.

Always work tent stitches so that they slant from left to right. Start at the top left-hand corner of the design, bring the needle from the back to the front of the canvas (see arrow on Fig 1), leaving about 2–3cm (¾–1¼in) of thread at the back. This will be sewn in when the first few stitches are made. Do not make knots to secure the thread as this will leave unsightly bumps under the finished work. Take the needle diagonally up to the right, pushing it down through the next hole in the row above: then bring it back through the hole immediately below, as shown in Fig 1. Work the rows straight from left to right, so that the stitches are vertical on the wrong side of the canvas (see Fig 3).

When working small areas of a design, stitch to the end of each row, then turn the canvas upside down to work the next row. Alternatively, simply stitch from right to left, without turning the canvas, as shown in Fig 2. The end of the finished thread should be worked in on the wrong side of the work, as shown in Fig 3.

You may prefer to work by stitching areas of one colour rather than working row by row. If two areas of the same colour are close together, you may jump across a few stitches, but if not, finish off the thread and start again. Check the number of stitches you take against the chart carefully, as an unnoticed mistake will affect the whole design.

When using stranded cottons you will need to separate the strands of cotton first, and then re-combine the required amount of strands together. This helps keep the threads from twisting around each other as you stitch and ensure sufficient coverage.

Cut all lengths of thread approximately 38cm (15in) long for working details or motifs, and 51cm (20in) for large areas of background. Do not be tempted to use longer lengths as they will tangle and knot. If you find that your thread does become twisted, hold the needlepoint up and let the needle and thread hang down to allow it to untwist. Do not continue working with twisted thread, as it will appear thinner and will not cover the canvas properly.

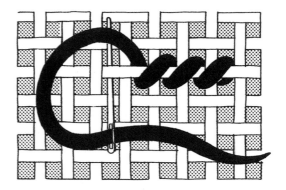

Fig 1

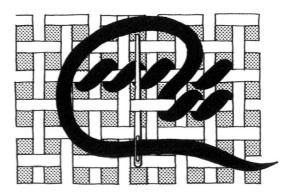

Fig 2

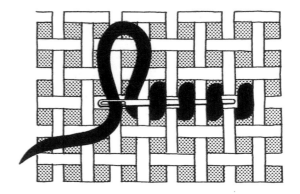

Fig 3

STRETCHING NEEDLEPOINT

If you haven't worked your embroidery on a frame you will probably find that the finished needlepoint has pulled slightly out of shape, in which case it will require stretching before it can be made up. If you are having the embroidery framed this will be done for you. However, it is easy to do oneself. You will need a firm board slightly larger than your canvas, some rust-proof tacks, a sheet of blotting paper and a sheet of graph paper slightly larger than your needlepoint design. With reference to Figs 4a and 4b complete the following steps.

Fig 4b

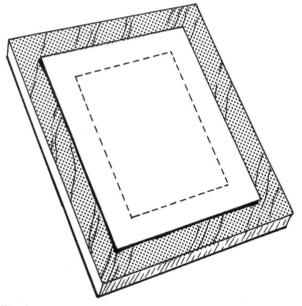

Fig 4a

1 Cover the board with graph paper, then draw the outline shape on the paper, about 5cm (2in) larger than your piece of needlepoint.

2 Cut the blotting paper to the same size as the worked section of needlepoint, then place it on top of the graph paper to absorb the moisture when the needlepoint is dampened.

3 Pin out the needlepoint face downwards on top of the blotting paper using the rust-proof tacks. Pull the canvas gently into shape, using the squares on the graph paper to check that it is correctly aligned. Pin all edges, placing the tacks 0.5cm (¼in) apart.

4 Using a damp cloth, gently dampen the needlepoint with water, taking great care not to make it too wet: on no account soak the canvas. Then leave it to dry. Dampening the needlepoint in this way softens the gum which is used to stiffen the canvas threads, and they will re-set in the correct position as they dry.

5 After the needlepoint has completely dried out and reset – which may take up to three weeks – the tacks may be carefully removed. If the needlepoint has been pulled badly out of shape, the stretching process may need to be repeated.

MOUNTING NEEDLEPOINT EMBROIDERIES

Before mounting your needlepoint picture prior to framing, ensure that it is straight and flat, stretching it if required, then follow the steps below.

1 Cut your mounting board to the required size for your finished picture, making sure that you will have 4–5cm (1½–2in) of surplus canvas extending all round the board. Trim the canvas to this size, making it altogether 7.5–10cm (3–4in) wider and deeper than the board.

2 To stretch your needlepoint embroidery over the mounting board, place it face down on a clean flat surface and position the board centrally on top. Rest a heavy book or similar weight in the centre, to prevent the board moving. You may also find it helpful to use double-sided adhesive tape on the right side of the board before placing it on the back of the embroidery, as this will ensure there is no movement. Mitre each corner very carefully, cutting the canvas just a fraction away from the corner of the board (see Fig 5).

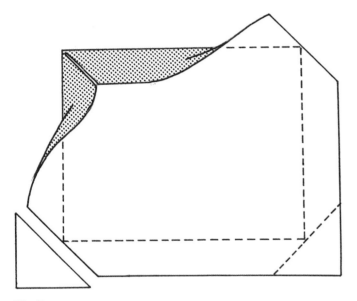

Fig 5

3 Fold one edge of the fabric over the mounting board (checking to make sure that the thread line of the canvas is absolutely straight), and secure it with pins along the edge of the board. Fix the opposite edge in the same way, again checking that the canvas is straight and taut on the board. Use masking tape to secure the edges of the canvas smoothly to the back of the mounting board, and then remove the pins. Repeat this procedure for the remaining two edges.

Alternatively, there is a specially prepared board available (called Press-On board) that simplifies the job considerably whilst ensuring accurate positioning and correctly aligned edges. These self-stick mounting boards are available in various sizes, from most large department stores and good craft shops. To use them, prepare your embroidery as before and cut the Press-On mounting board to size, as before. Peel the backing off and place it centrally over the back of the needlepoint, with the edges straight to the thread line of the canvas. When you are satisfied, press down very hard over the entire surface. If necessary, turn the whole thing over care-fully and press the canvas down onto the board to ensure it is firmly stuck. With the right side down again, mitre the corners (as above). Fold excess canvas neatly over each side and tape it to the back of the board.

Your needlepoint picture is now ready to be framed. Unless you have experience in this craft, you will find it more satisfactory to take your work to a professional framer. If there is to be glass in the frame, you will probably find that the non-reflective type is worth the additional expense.

PATCHWORK-STYLE ❧ CUSHIONS ❧

*T*his striking set of four cushions was initially inspired by the colourful traditional patchwork patterns often used for cushions. I thought it would be very effective to show the cats against these pretty backgrounds.

MATERIALS *(for each cushion)*

- 10 count double-thread canvas 48.5cm (19in) square
- Contrasting backing fabric 40.5cm (16in) square (of a similar weight to the finished needlepoint)
- DMC tapestry wool as shown on the chart
- Tapestry needle size 18
- Matching sewing thread
- Cushion pad 35.5cm (14in) square
- Cord and tassels to trim if required

Finished size

34cm (13½in) square

1 Mount the canvas in a frame following the directions on page 10. Following the appropriate chart, stitch the design centrally on the canvas, according to the stitching techniques on page 11.

You may find that your needlepoint will require stretching before being made up, if so see page 12.

2 Once the needlepoint is complete, trim away the excess canvas, leaving a 2.5cm (1in) border of unworked canvas all round.

3 Place the needlepoint and backing fabric together, right sides facing, and machine stitch around three sides, stitching as close as possible to the worked area.

4 Snip off any excess canvas across the corners, press the seams open and turn right side out.

5 Insert the cushion pad, then turn in the canvas and backing at the open end and slipstitch neatly together, level with the edge of the needlepoint. Sew braided cord or piping neatly around the edge, adding tassels to the corners if you wish.

Four different cats inspired these delightful patchwork cushions: Isis, Jo Jo, Scoot, and Mr Tibbs

ISIS

Isis was a beautiful Egyptian Mau belonging to a friend of mine who lived in a small village in the Hertfordshire countryside. He was a marvellous hunter, and would disappear early in the morning to roam the open countryside in search of his prey, which he would dutifully bring home for his 'master'. His territory was vast and stories of him being spotted by local farmers from the next village were common. He was a very intelligent and proud creature, some thought him rather aloof, but he wasn't at all. He was just very wary of strangers, only allowing people he knew well to stroke him.

ISIS CUSHION

	DMC Tapestry Wool	No of skeins		DMC Tapestry Wool	No of skeins
■	Noir	1	I	7518	1
·	Blanc	1	∩	7772	1
⊞	7820	1	N	7110	1
⋈	7797	2	□	7771	1
∴	7437	1	⌐	7911	1
O	7741	2	♪	7545	1
+	7606	1			
4	7245	1			
Z	7242	1			
∧	7711	1			
≢	7995	1			
−	7996	2			
✳	7344	1			
V	7341	2			
F	7435	1			
U	7433	1			
↖	7135	1			
H	7605	1			
⊥	7317	1			
◆	7914	1			
▨	7469	2			
X	7479	3			
▤	7845	2			
‖	7846	3			
\	7579	2			
⁒	7503	1			
T	7168	1			
S	7124	1			
Ø	7640	1			
I	7313	1			
✚	7257	1			
<	7304	1			
→	7861	1			

JO JO

*Jo Jo was a British Blue cat who
adopted me many years ago, when her
previous owners decided to move and
not take her with them. It was terribly
sad to see her shut out of her home,
miaowing and scratching at the front
door trying to get in. I began feeding
her and after a few days she began
coming into my house for short periods,
and eventually decided to stay. She was
a very sweet and gentle cat, who would
follow me about all over the house,
sitting on my lap whenever I sat down.
She was also a very good mouser and
as I had fields at the back of the house,
she was always coming home with
various rodent 'presents' for me, which
was most unpleasant. This act, however,
meant that she regarded me as one of
her family. So as not to upset her, I
would praise her for her kind act, and
then quietly dispose of the poor creature
when Jo Jo was not around!*

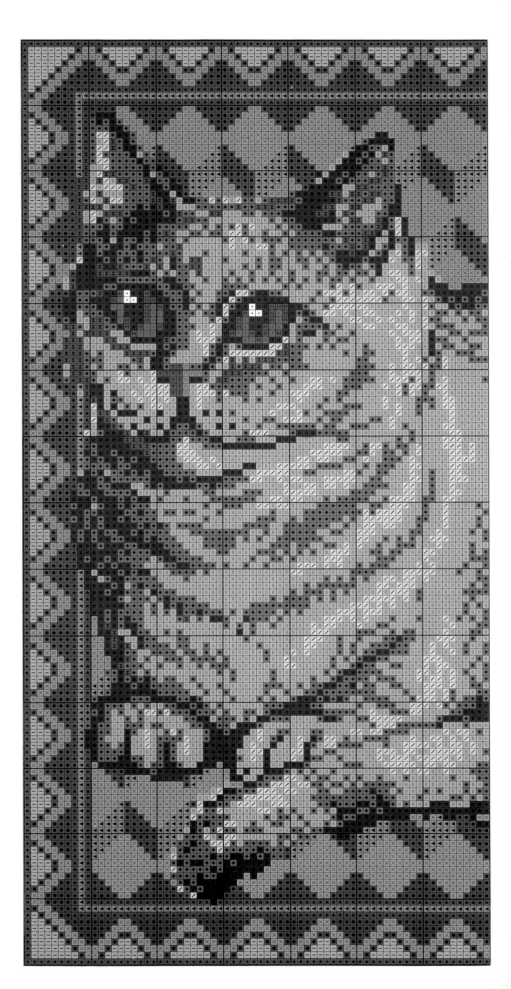

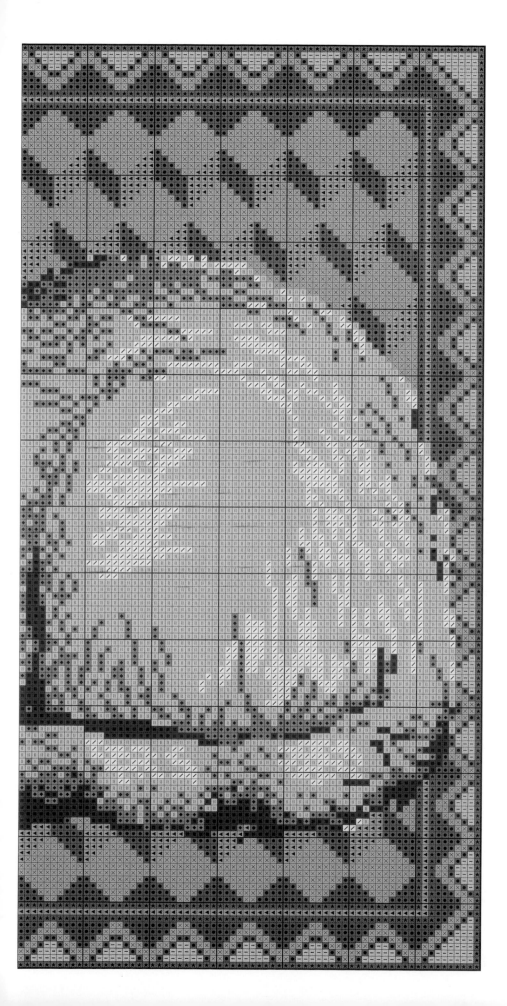

JO JO CUSHION

	DMC Tapestry Wool	No of skeins
⊠	7711	4
●	7242	4
—	7772	2
◀	7370	2
·	Blanc	1
★	7245	2
‖	7558	5
◆	7626	3
╱	7715	3
⊠	7713	1
⠒	7726	1
H	7444	1
■	Noir	1
∩	7287	1
T	7339	1

SCOOT

Scoot, a Tortoiseshell-and-white Shorthair belonging to a friend of mine, got her name because she used to scoot after anything that moved! My friend lived in a flat, so Scoot didn't go out very much, and practised her hunting skills on inanimate objects in the flat! Nothing was safe. She actually used to retrieve things too; a habit which begun when she was quite young. We were sitting round the flat eating some sweets, screwing up the wrappers and throwing them into the waste paper basket, when Scoot ran across the room, pounced head first into the basket, and reappeared with a sweet wrapper in her mouth. Finding this very amusing, we encouraged her to bring us the wrappers by giving her cat treats, and eventually she used to perform this trick at will.

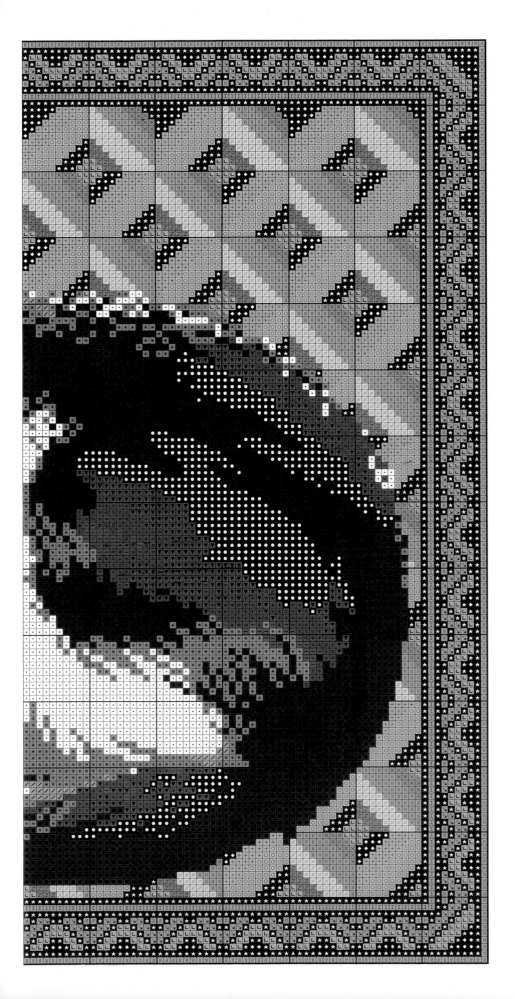

SCOOT CUSHION

	DMC Tapestry Wool	No of skeins
■	Noir	5
·	Blanc	2
‖	7711	2
★	7797	4
I	7952	1
◆	7911	1
+	7773	1
○	7798	2
✳	7287	2
／	7617	1
％	7958	1
✕	7314	1
Ζ	7956	1
L	7772	2
▦	7922	1
▼	7700	1
◖	7458	1
▬	7918	1
⋂	7175	1
✖	7705	1
T	7840	1
↘	7709	1
V	7725	1
S	7740	1
N	7445	1
▢	7919	1

MR TIBBS

Mr Tibbs was a huge Brown Tabby Shorthair who used to come and visit me to be fed and pampered. I don't know if he actually belonged to anybody, or whether he just used to 'visit' various homes to be fed and watered. He used to make himself at home nevertheless. He would jump up on to the armchair and lay there for hours quite still, though not asleep, and watch everything going on around him in a rapture of attention. Caresses were tolerated by him occasionally but usually when he wanted feeding. After a few hours, he would get up, stretch, and disappear out through the cat flap.

MR TIBBS CUSHION

	DMC Tapestry Wool	No of skeins
▨	Noir	3
⊥	7293	1
◈	7558	1
·	Blanc	1
●	7820	1
✕	7797	1
⁒	7807	1
I	7313	1
+	7555	1
→	7798	1
⊿	7342	1
∅	7911	1
▲	7906	1
⊞	7915	1
↓	7255	1
◧	7257	3
⊕	7375	1
≡	7640	2
▼	7139	1
∨	7151	2
↖	7804	1
◎	7135	1
Z	7895	1
⊥	7708	1
▽	7341	1
✳	7346	1
◆	7479	3
T	7951	1
✕	7477	2
‖	7463	2
╱	7460	1
⌊	7626	1

FRAMED MINIATURE DUO

These delightful miniature pictures will make an attractive addition to your home, whether you display them singly or as a pair. Either of the designs would make a lovely gift. The cats shown with their kittens are a Blue Tabby Persian and a Chocolate-Point Himalayan.

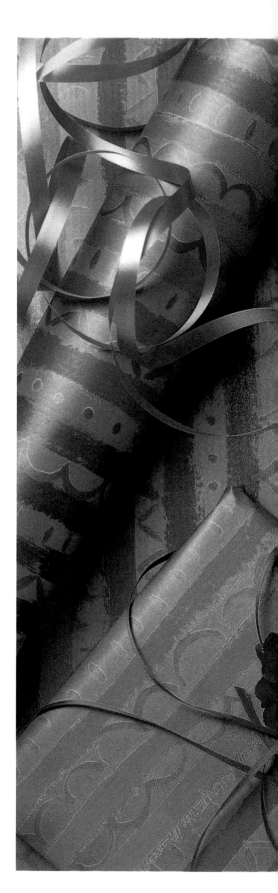

MATERIALS *(for one picture)*

- 14 count single-thread canvas 20.5cm (8in) square
- DMC six-strand stranded embroidery cotton as shown on the chart
- Tapestry needle size 24
- Heavyweight iron-on interfacing
- One round brass frame 15cm (6in) in diameter (see Suppliers page 127)

Finished size

15cm (6in) diameter

1 Mount the canvas in a frame, following the directions on page 10. Following the appropriate chart from page 26 or 27, stitch the design centrally onto your piece of canvas using the required number of strands throughout (see page 8) and according to the stitching techniques on page 11.

2 If your finished needlepoint embroidery requires stretching, see page 12.

3 Iron the interfacing on to the wrong side of the embroidery to prevent the canvas fraying.

4 Carefully dismantle all parts of the picture frame and use the template provided with the frame to draw around your design, making sure that it is central. Very carefully cut out your embroidery along that line.

5 Place the acetate back in the frame. Put your embroidery in position, then the thin card and finally the backing. Your picture is now complete.

These charming miniatures show a Blue Tabby Persian (top) and a Chocolate-point Himalayan (bottom)

BLUE TABBY PERSIAN

	DMC Stranded Cotton		DMC Stranded Cotton
▦	310	▶	3685
●	317	S	603
○	318	✕	958
↘	415	I	725
·	Blanc	V	321
↘	208		

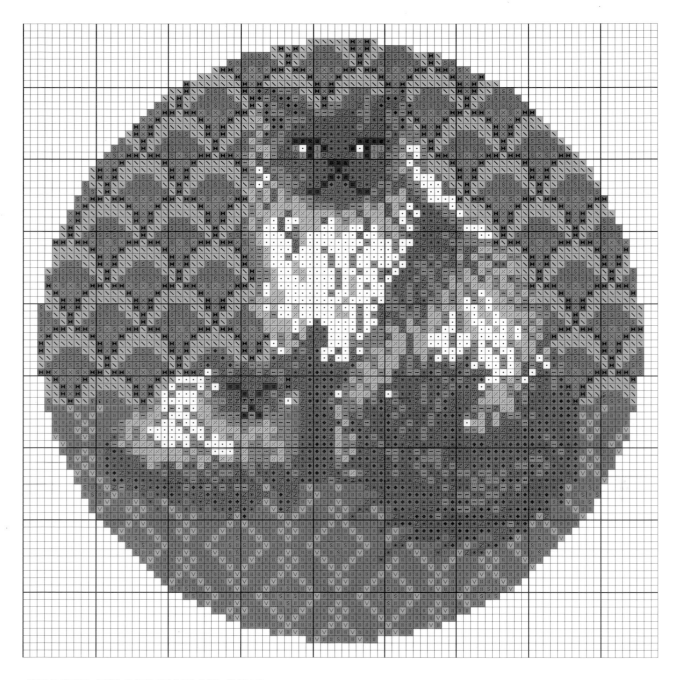

CHOCOLATE-POINT HIMALAYAN

	DMC Stranded Cotton		DMC Stranded Cotton		DMC Stranded Cotton
■	310	✳	801	V	3755
—	3828	S	743	II	3746
◆	3031	✕	958		
⁒	738	⋈	333		
·	Blanc	I	826		
Z	434	＼	799		

LEMA'S FIRST LITTER

*T*his sewing box is ideal for displaying this charming picture of Lema and her kittens. Lema chose my bed to give birth to her first litter of kittens, which was quite a surprise! A beautiful tabby and white cat, she gave birth to five lovely kittens identical to herself. She would carry them out to the garden one at a time and supervise their play amongst the flowers. Exhausted, the kittens would cuddle up to their mum for a nap in the sun.

MATERIALS

- 10 count double-thread canvas 49.5 x 40.5cm (19½ x 16in)
- DMC tapestry wool as shown
- Tapestry needle size 18
- Calico 39.5 x 30.5cm (15½ x 12in) (optional)
- Self-cover sewing box (see Suppliers page 127)
- 6mm (¼in) rust-proof tacks or a staple gun

Finished size
39.5 x 30.5cm (15½ x 12in)

1 Mount the canvas in a frame, following the directions on page 10. Following the chart, on pages 30 and 31, stitch the design according to the stitching techniques on page 11. As this design is quite large it may require stretching after completion, if so see page 12.

2 Complete your needlepoint design centrally on the canvas, leaving a 5cm (2in) border of unworked canvas all around.

3 Remove the top of the sewing box by undoing the screws, which are recessed under the frame. Put the screws in a safe place.

4 Lay your needlepoint right side down on a flat surface and place the pad face down in the centre so that there is an equal amount of canvas showing on all sides.

5 Press the pad down on to the canvas along one of the long edges. Kneel on it or ask a friend to help you. Bring the canvas over the edge and secure it in place with the rust-proof tacks or a staple gun.

Keep the canvas straight as you work, placing the tacks or staples in the centre then evenly spacing them out to each end approximately 2.5cm (1in) apart. Repeat the process along the other long edge, pulling the canvas tightly and evenly into place.

6 Squeeze the pad down over the first short edge and fasten it in place as before with either tacks or staples. Mitre the folds of canvas in the corners to give a neat appearance on the right side, then repeat the process on the other short edge.

7 At this stage you could glue or sew a piece of calico or similar material under the pad to neatly cover the tacked edges. Replace the top of the sewing box, gently pressing it in the corners where the fit will be tight. Rescrew the pad to the frame.

This sewing box is part of a beautiful range of self-upholster decorative furniture that is available from craft suppliers and department stores. It is designed to take a needlework design measuring 39.5 x 30.5cm (15½ x 12in)

LEMA'S FIRST LITTER

	DMC Tapestry Wool	No of skeins			DMC Tapestry Wool	No of skeins
	Noir	1	÷		7191	1
•	Blanc	2	F		7853	1
–	7558	1	★		7519	1
⁒	7626	1	∧		7455	1
▲	7408	2	╱		7166	1
V	7584	1	⊠		7700	1
L	7364	1	◺		7421	1
X	7915	1	!		7543	1
H	7906	1				
◣	7434	1				
○	7436	1				
⊞	7947	1				
◩	7666	1				
4	7110	1				
S	7852	1				
✳	7385	2				
+	7954	1				
Z	7243	1				
∅	7798	1				
:	7799	1				
◉	7535	1				
●	7469	3				
N	7466	3				
‖	7472	1				
▫	7762	1				
∩	7851	1				
T	7124	1				
◥	7802	1				
↓	7548	1				
⌐	7205	1				

❧ PEEPING TOM ❧

*T*he cheeky cat in this picture looks just as though he is peeping
through a small window. What mischief can he be thinking up?
Perhaps he has just seen a mouse scurry past!

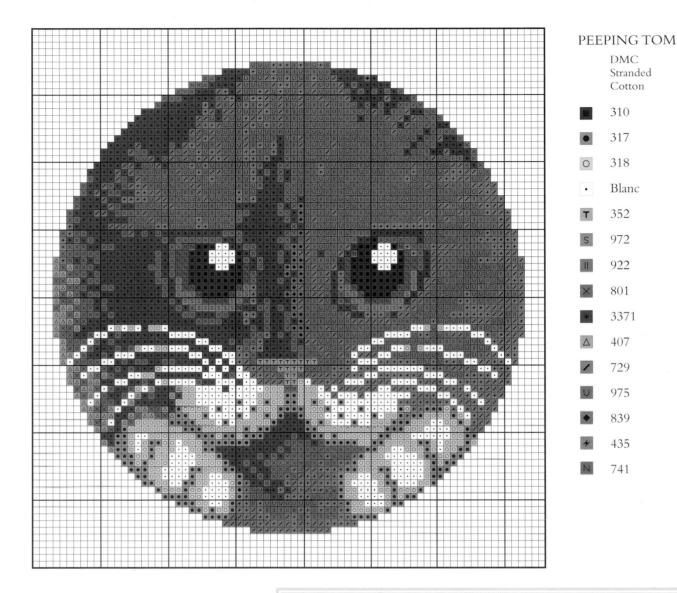

PEEPING TOM

DMC
Stranded
Cotton

■	310
●	317
○	318
·	Blanc
T	352
S	972
II	922
✕	801
✳	3371
△	407
╱	729
U	975
◆	839
⚡	435
N	741

1 Mount the canvas in a frame, following the directions on page 10. Following the chart above, stitch the design centrally onto your piece of canvas, according to the stitching techniques on page 11, using three strands throughout (see page 8).

2 If the finished embroidery requires stretching before being mounted for framing, see page 12.

3 To mount your embroidery ready for framing, see page 12.

MATERIALS

- 18 count single-thread canvas 28cm (11in) square
- Firm mounting board 20.5cm (8in) square
- DMC six-strand stranded cotton as shown on the chart

- Tapestry needle size 26
- Masking tape
- Picture frame of your choice

Finished size

10cm (4in) diameter

MORRIS-STYLE
❦ BELL PULL ❦

*T*he *inspiration for this sophisticated design came from the wonderful William Morris*
tapestries of the late 1800s. His use of rich colours, swirling leaves and the addition
of lush fruits and flowers, gave us the idea for this traditional-style bell pull.

MATERIALS

- 10 count double-thread canvas
  114.5 x 30.5cm (45 x 12in)
- Backing fabric (such as calico)
  111.5 x 23cm (44 x 9in)
- DMC tapestry wool as shown
  on the chart
- Tapestry needle size 18
- Brass bell pull ends for a
  design 20.5cm (8in) wide
- Matching sewing thread

Finished size

19.5 x 104cm (7¾ x 41in)

Detail of the bell pull

1 Mount the canvas in a frame following the directions on page 10. Following the chart on pages 36–39, stitch the design centrally onto the canvas according to the stitching techniques on page 11.

2 As this design is quite large, it may require stretching after completion, if so see page 12.

3 Once the needlepoint is complete, trim away any excess canvas, leaving a 1.25cm (½in) seam allowance on the long sides of the embroidery and 4cm (1½in) on the short ends.

4 The backing fabric should be the same width but 2.5cm (1in) longer than the canvas. Place the embroidery and fabric right sides together, with the backing 1.25cm (½in) above and below the canvas. Pin, tack and stitch the sides together, turn to the right side and press. Put an end through the bell pull and turn over. Make a 0.5cm (¼in) turning on the backing fabric and turn over the ends of canvas. Machine stitch in place and then stitch down onto the backing fabric using slipstitch.

MORRIS-STYLE BELL PULL

	DMC Tapestry Wool	No of skeins
★	Noir	1
·	Blanc	2
▲	7797	4
■	7823	8
=	7433	2
○	7741	1

	DMC Tapestry Wool	No of skeins
✕	7911	6
╱	7604	5
S	7711	1
Σ	7243	1
L	7946	1
T	7178	1

	DMC Tapestry Wool	No of skeins
❙	7175	1
H	7340	1
→	7875	1
⊞	7666	1
Z	7782	1
●	7497	1
⁴	7401	1

	DMC Tapestry Wool	No of skeins
N	7713	1
⁄	7618	1
□	7715	1
U	7466	1
⊡	7467	1
F	7232	1
∅	7176	1

MORRIS-STYLE BELL PULL

DMC Tapestry Wool	No of skeins		DMC Tapestry Wool	No of skeins		DMC Tapestry Wool	No of skeins		DMC Tapestry Wool	No of skeins
★ Noir	1	✗	7911	6	⌧ 7175	1	N 7713	1
• Blanc	2	╱	7604	5	H 7340	1	⊘ 7618	1
▲ 7797	4	S	7711	1	→ 7875	1	☐ 7715	1
■ 7823	8	Σ	7243	1	‡ 7666	1	U 7466	1
= 7433	2	L	7946	1	Z 7782	1	⊡ 7467	1
⊙ 7741	1	T	7178	1	● 7497	1	F 7232	1
					4 7401	1	⦸ 7176	1

BUTTERFLY WATCHING

*This pretty design of Tiffany watching a butterfly was
initially inspired by a photograph of her in the garden
watching the butterflies on the flowers. Then Leannda came up
with the brilliant idea of including the Art Nouveau background,
resulting in this delightful picture.*

MATERIALS

- 10 count double-thread canvas
  72.5 x 52.5cm (28½ x 20¾in)
- Firm mounting board 62 x
  42.5cm (24½ x 16¾in)
- DMC tapestry wool as shown
  on the chart
- Tapestry needle size 18
- Masking tape
- Picture frame of your choice

Finished size

42 x 61cm (16½ x 24in)

1 Mount the canvas in a frame,
following the directions on page
10. Following the chart on pages
42–45, stitch the design centrally
onto the canvas according to the
stitching techniques described on
page 11.

2 As this design is quite large, it
may require stretching before it is
ready to be mounted for framing, if
so see page 12.

3 To mount your needlepoint
embroidery ready for framing, see
page 12.

BUTTERFLY WATCHING

	DMC Tapestry Wool	No of skeins
■	Noir	1
·	Blanc	2
▤	7437	1
↑	7360	1
▽	7124	1
S	7852	1
╲	7725	1
●	7906	12
Ⅱ	7943	4
⦂	7911	7
⁒	7382	6
T	7304	1
⤨	7766	2
▼	7245	2
✕	7242	1
◇	7711	2
◣	7506	3
◟	7503	2
◪	7515	2
N	7497	1
∩	7465	1
⌀	7459	2

	DMC Tapestry Wool	No of skeins
	Noir	1
	Blanc	2
	7437	1
	7360	1
	7124	1
S	7852	1
	7725	1
	7906	12
	7943	4
	7911	7
	7382	6
T	7304	1
	7766	2
	7245	2
X	7242	1
	7711	2
	7506	3
	7503	2
	7515	2
N	7497	1
	7465	1
	7459	2

CHRISTMAS STOCKING
❧ CATS ❧

*W*hat cat lover could possibly resist this gorgeous Christmas stocking bulging with presents!
The design features five different British Shorthair varieties, starting at the top with the
Red Tabby, followed by the British Blue, Tortoiseshell-and-white, Black-and-white Bi-coloured, and
finally the Brown Tabby. With all the holly, bells, baubles, ribbons and bows,
who could fail to have a merry Christmas!

1 Mount the canvas in a frame following the directions on page 10. Following the chart, on pages 48–49, stitch the design centrally onto the canvas, according to the stitching techniques on page 11. As this design is quite large, it may require stretching after completion, if so, see page 12.

2 When the needlepoint is complete, trim the canvas, leaving a seam allowance of 1.25cm (½in) all round the embroidery. Cut the backing fabric to the same size and from the lining fabric cut two pieces also of the same size.

3 Pin, tack and stitch the embroidery to the backing fabric, right sides together, leaving the top open. Clip the curves and turn to the right side.

4 Place the embroidery inside the lining right sides together, then stitch the tops together. Turn the stocking through the opening in the stocking foot, slipstitch the opening together, and push the lining into the stocking.

5 Trim with the contrasting coloured cord, adding the tassel at the back of the open end.

MATERIALS

- 10 count double-thread canvas 56 x 40.5cm (22 x 16in)
- Contrasting backing fabric (of a similar weight to the finished needlepoint), same size as the canvas
- Cotton fabric for the lining 56 x 81.5cm (22 x 32in)
- DMC tapestry wool as shown on the chart
- DMC fil or foncé gold thread
- Tapestry needle size 18
- Matching sewing thread
- Contrasting 5mm (¼in) cord to trim, 1.8m (2yd)
- One contrasting colour tassel

Finished size
47 x 37.5cm (18½ x 14½in)

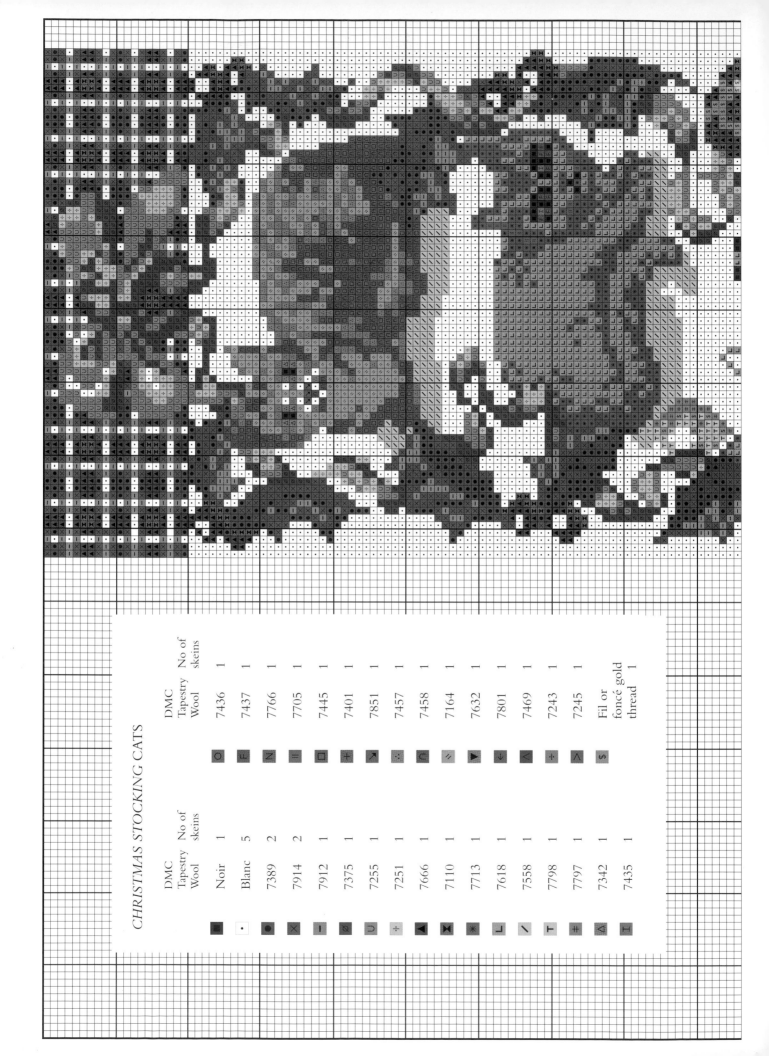

CHRISTMAS STOCKING CATS

DMC Tapestry Wool		No of skeins
Noir	■	1
Blanc	·	5
7389	●	2
7914	×	2
7912	I	1
7375	Ø	1
7255	∪	1
7251	÷	1
7666	◀	1
7110	⋈	1
7713	*	1
7618	⌐	1
7558	\	1
7798	T	1
7797	+	1
7342	◁	1
7435	⊤	1

DMC Tapestry Wool		No of skeins
7436	O	1
7437	F	1
7766	N	1
7705	=	1
7445	□	1
7401	+	1
7851	↗	1
7457	∴	1
7458	∪	1
7164	∻	1
7632	▶	1
7801	↓	1
7469	<	1
7243	÷	1
7245	∧	1
Fil or foncé gold thread	$	1

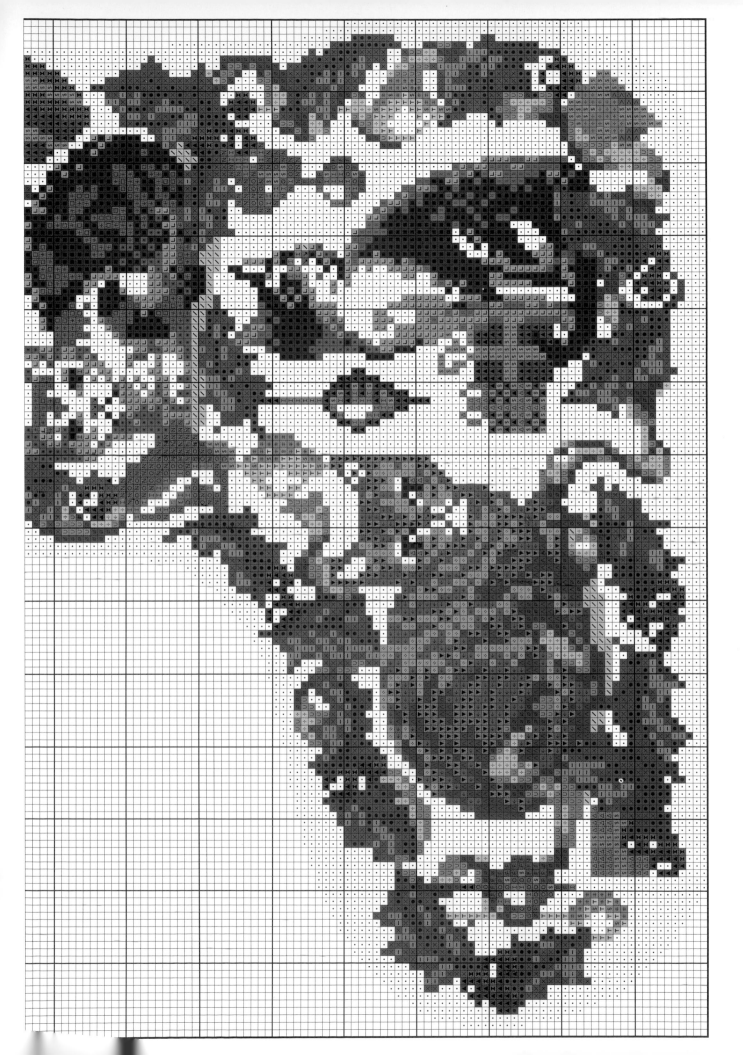

CELESTIAL CAT ❧ RUG ❧

*C*ats are expert sleepers, sleeping away approximately two-thirds of their lives and Leannda's cat Paisley is no exception! Warmth, security and a full stomach provokes sleep in Paisley at almost any time of the day. This enchanting rug features him asleep and dreaming of all his wonderful secret exploits.

MATERIALS

- 10 count double-thread canvas 59 x 84cm (23¼ x 33in)
- Calico for the backing 54 x 79cm (21¼ x 31in)
- DMC tapestry wool as shown on the chart
- Tapestry needle size 18
- Matching sewing thread
- Contrasting upholstery fring-ing to trim 104cm (41in)

Finished size
49 x 73.5cm (19¼ x 29in)

1 Mount the canvas in a frame, following the directions on page 10. Following the chart on pages 52–55, stitch the design centrally onto the canvas, according to the stitching techniques on page 11. As this is a large design, it may require stretching after completion, if so, see page 12.

2 Once the needlepoint is complete, trim any excess canvas, leaving 2.5cm (1in) of unworked canvas on each long side (above and below the design) and 4cm (1½in) on each short edge.

3 Place embroidery and backing fabric right sides together. Pin and tack the two long edges, allowing a 2.5cm (1in) seam allowance. Machine stitch as close to the embroidery as you can. Trim the corners and turn to the right side.

4 Turn in a 2.5cm (1in) seam allowance on each short end and press. This will leave you with 1.25cm (½in) of unworked canvas along each side of the embroidery. Machine stitch 0.5cm (¼in) from the edge on both sides.

5 Pin and tack the fringing to the right side of the rug onto the unworked canvas as close to the embroidery as you can, turning 1.25cm (½in) over to the back at each end. Machine stitch into place. Remove pins and tacking.

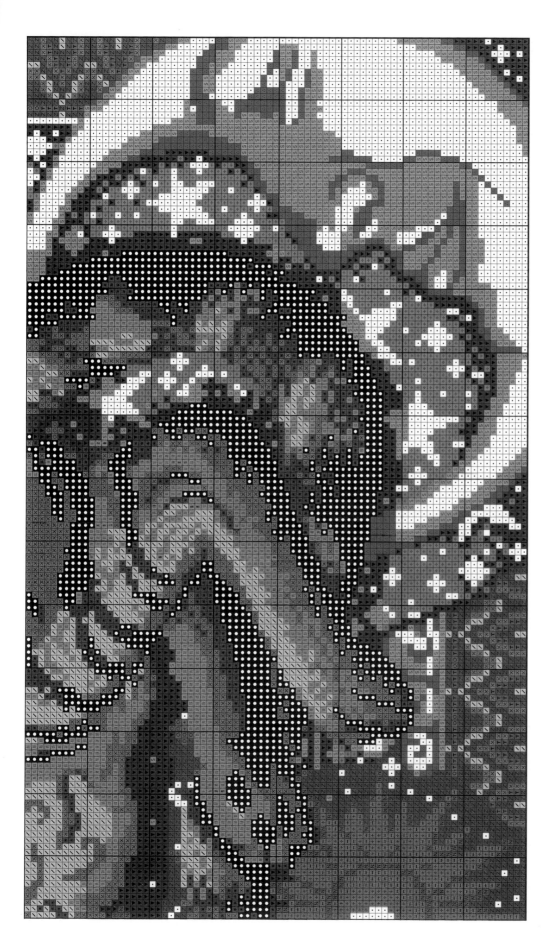

CELESTIAL CAT RUG

	DMC Tapestry Wool	No of skeins
■	Noir	1
·	Blanc	5
◖	7533	8
✕	7780	6
✳	7459	4
‖	7506	3
╱	7739	3
▼	7823	5
Z	7820	8
÷	7797	2
+	7786	5
–	7782	3
N	7401	2
↑	7470	2
S	7618	3
▪	7713	2
●	7360	1
O	7436	1
T	7807	1
U	7761	1

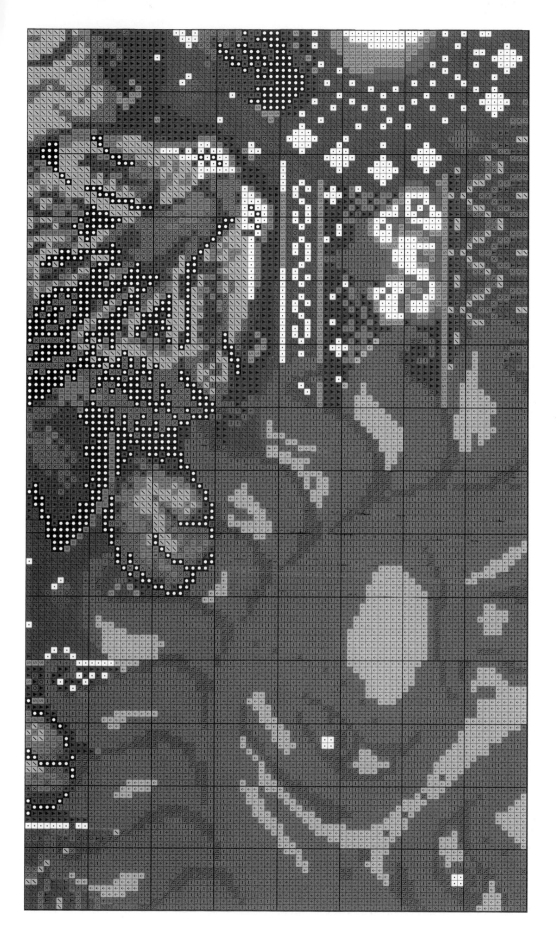

	DMC Tapestry Wool	No of skeins
■	Noir	1
·	Blanc	5
◉	7533	8
✕	7780	6
✳	7459	4
‖	7506	3
╱	7739	3
▼	7823	5
Z	7820	8
÷	7797	2
+	7786	5
–	7782	3
N	7401	2
↑	7470	2
S	7618	3
⁜	7713	2
●	7360	1
○	7436	1
T	7807	1
U	7761	1

FIGURINE DOORSTOP

*T*he inspiration for this design came from the old Staffordshire figures popular in the late 1800s. We thought it would be a marvellous idea to have a design of a sitting cat in the book, but we didn't want another shaped cushion (although one could omit the weight and use it as such) so I came up with the idea of a doorstop. Then came the problem of how to make it heavy enough to hold a door open. I was visiting a friend when I saw a few measuring scale weights in the kitchen. I picked one up realising it was just what I need. 'Can I have this please?' I asked with great excitement. My friend asked what I wanted it for. I replied, 'For one of my embroidery projects.' He looked very perplexed but gave it to me without further question!

MATERIALS

- 10 count double-thread canvas 42 x 35.5cm (16½ x 14in)
- Backing fabric 58.5 x 35.5cm (23 x 14in) (in a similar weight to the finished needlepoint)
- DMC tapestry wool as shown on the chart
- Tapestry needle size 18
- Matching sewing thread
- Tracing paper
- Kapok or washable polyester filling
- Old kitchen scales weight (or similar heavy object)
- Scrap pieces of lightweight fabric to cover weight

Finished size

19 x 32cm (7½ x 12½in)

1 Mount the canvas in a frame following the directions on page 10. Following the chart, on page 58, stitch the design centrally onto the canvas, according to the stitching techniques on page 11. The design may require stretching after completion, if so, see page 12.

2 Once the needlepoint is complete, trim away any excess canvas leaving 1.25cm (½in) of unworked canvas all round the embroidery. From the backing fabric, cut a piece the same shape as the embroidery including the seam allowance. Trace the pattern piece for the base, and then, from the remaining backing fabric, cut a piece for the base.

3 Place the embroidery and backing piece right sides together then pin and tack. Trim the ears to points and clip all the curves to help turn properly. Machine stitch all round as close to the embroidery as possible, leaving the bottom open. Remove the pins and tacking stitches. Pin and tack the base to the embroidery and machine stitch into place, leaving a 10cm (4in) gap for turning.

4 Turn the cat to the right side and stuff very firmly, making sure the stuffing is pushed right up into the ears. When the body is almost full, cover the weight with the scrap pieces of lightweight fabric and place it inside the body. Add more stuffing, ensuring that the weight is well covered. Slipstitch the remaining side of the base to the backing fabric, gently adding the last pieces of stuffing as you go.

Trace the actual-size template shown in blue on this page to make the shape of doorstop base

FIGURINE DOORSTOP

	DMC Tapestry Wool	No of skeins
◼	Noir	1
⁒	Blanc	1
◪	7469	2
✕	7458	2
▯	7234	1
·	7739	3
T	7124	1
S	7918	1
●	7796	1
◺	7798	1
÷	7799	1
◯	7922	1
V	7700	2
╱	7466	3

EGYPTIAN CATS PICTURE

	DMC Stranded Cotton
◼	310
·	Blanc
◯	725
╱	676
▯	943
÷	996
●	798
◪	433
V	783
◇	800
✕	Fil or foncé gold thread

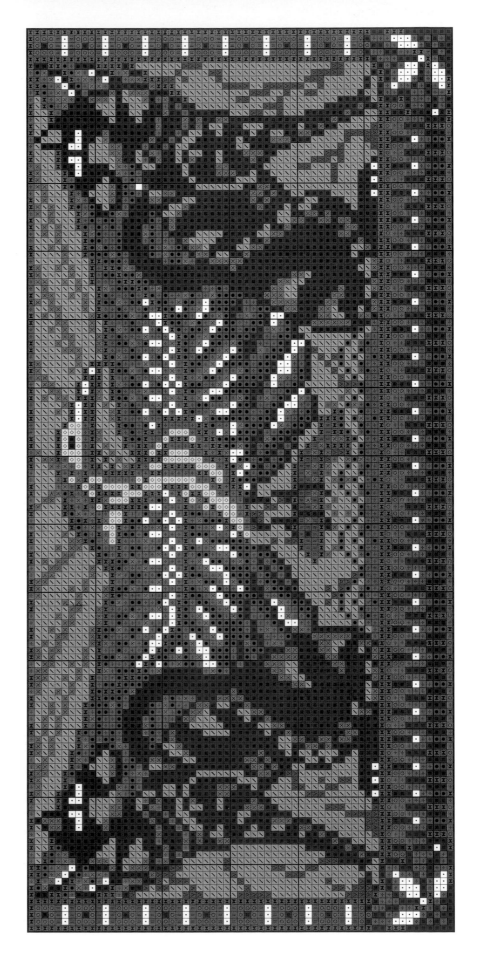

EGYPTIAN CATS
❧ PICTURE ❧

*T*he inspiration for this design came from delicate ancient Egyptian papyrus paintings found in the British Museum. The cat was much revered in Egypt, in fact the earliest recorded picture of a cat was painted in an Egyptian tomb about 2,600BC. Egyptian deities were often depicted as cats, or with a cat's head. The Egyptian word for cat was mau, which originated from the cat's voice. The cat was so venerated throughout Egypt that it became sacred and it was a crime punishable by death to eat or kill one. Paintings of the time show that the Egyptians were very fond of their household cats. Both temple and household cats were given a formal burial when they died and were usually mummified. Elaborate coffins and mummy cases have survived to this day.

MATERIALS
- 14 count single-thread canvas 21.5 x 34.25cm (8½ x 13½in)
- Firm mounting board 11.5 x 24cm (4½ x 9½in)
- DMC six-strand stranded cotton as shown on the chart
- DMC Fil or foncé gold thread
- Tapestry needle size 24
- Masking tape
- Picture frame of your choice

Finished size
24 x 11.5cm (9½ x 4½in)

1 Mount the canvas in a frame following the directions on page 10. Following the chart on page 59 stitch the design centrally onto the canvas, using the required number of strands throughout (see page 8) and according to the stitching techniques on page 11.

2 If the embroidery requires stretching when you have finished stitching, see page 12.

3 To mount your needlepoint embroidery ready for framing, see page 12.

SLEEPY CAT CUSHIONS

This beautiful set of rectangular cushions depicts four different cat breeds asleep on a favourite rug. The idea for this set was to show the breed of cat against a background relating to its origin. The Siamese cat is shown on a Chinese rug, the Persian cat on a Persian rug, the Turkish Angora cat on a Turkish rug, and the British Tabby on a William Morris inspired rug. When choosing your backing fabric, bear in mind that you will need something of a similar weight to the finished needlepoint. Velvet, Dralon and other medium- to heavyweight curtain fabrics are ideal.

TO MAKE A RECTANGULAR CUSHION PAD

1 Cut two 35.5 x 48.5cm (14 x 19in) rectangles of calico. Pin the pieces together, right sides facing, and sew all round leaving an opening of about 10cm (4in) on one side. Clip the corners and turn to the right side.

2 Stuff the pad firmly, then turn in the raw edges of the opening and slipstitch together.

TO MAKE A CUSHION

3 Mount the canvas in a frame following the directions on page 10. Following the appropriate chart, stitch the design according to the stitching techniques on page 11.

4 When you have completed your needlepoint design centrally on the canvas, trim away the excess canvas, leaving a 2.5cm (1in) border of unworked canvas all round. You may find that your embroidery will require stretching before being made up, if so, see page 12.

5 To make up the cushion, place the needlepoint and backing fabric together, right sides facing, and machine stitch around two long sides and one short side, stitching as close as possible to the worked area.

6 Snip off any excess canvas across the corners, press the seams open and turn the cushion to the right side.

7 Insert the cushion pad, then turn in the canvas and backing at the open end and slipstitch neatly together, level with the edge of the needlepoint.

8 Braided cord or piping may be sewn neatly around the edges of the cushion, with tassels stitched to the corners for added effect.

MATERIALS *(for one cushion)*
- 10 count double-thread canvas 48.5 x 61cm (19 x 24in)
- Calico 50cm (19¾in) x 115cm (45in) wide
- Contrasting backing fabric 40.5 x 53.5cm (16 x 21in)
- DMC tapestry wool as shown on the chart
- Tapestry needle size 18
- Matching sewing thread
- Kapok or washable polyester filling
- Cord and tassels to trim if required

Finished size *(for each cushion)*
35.5 x 48.5cm (14 x 19in)

Clockwise from top right; the Turkish Angora, the British Tabby, the Persian and the Siamese

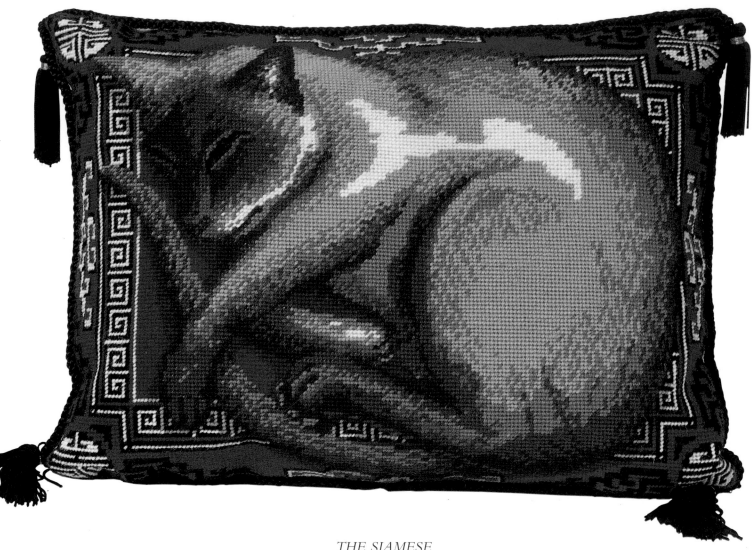

THE SIAMESE

The origins of the Siamese cat are uncertain but it is now accepted to be of Eastern origin. It may have originated in Thailand, according to an early (pre 1676) manuscript held in the National Bangkok Library. In 1794 a German naturalist reported a darker type of pointed cat east of the Caspian Sea.

The Siamese is slim and elegant with a long body, fine limbs with oval paws and a long, tapering tail. It has a long, triangular-shaped head with large pointed ears and oblique, almond-shaped, vivid blue eyes. The coat is shorthaired with a light ground colour and dark colourpoints – the points being the mask, ears, legs, feet and tail. These may be seal, blue, chocolate, lilac, red or cream. The cat also appears in tortoise-shell and tabby versions.

The temperament of the Siamese is different from any other breed as its general attitude can change radically from day to day. It is an intelligent cat with a genial and lively personality, a lovable companion, often bonding strongly with its owners and demanding much attention.

THE PERSIAN

Most of the longhaired pedigree cats today are descended from cats imported to Britain from Turkey and Persia in the late nineteenth century. It is thought that the Persian is descended from the Angora with evidence of this dating as far back as 1520.

The modern Persian, has a stout, massive body set on short, thick legs with large, round paws, and a short tail. Its head, set on a short thick neck, is broad and round with small round-tipped ears and a short snub nose. The eyes are large and expressive, with well-defined colour that harmonises with the coat. The coat is long and flowing over a thick undercoat with a full ruff around the face and between the front legs. The colour varieties are numerous, including solid colours such as black, white, blue, cream and red, and also bi-coloureds, vari-colours and various patterns. The Persian has a likeable temperament and is exceptionally affectionate.

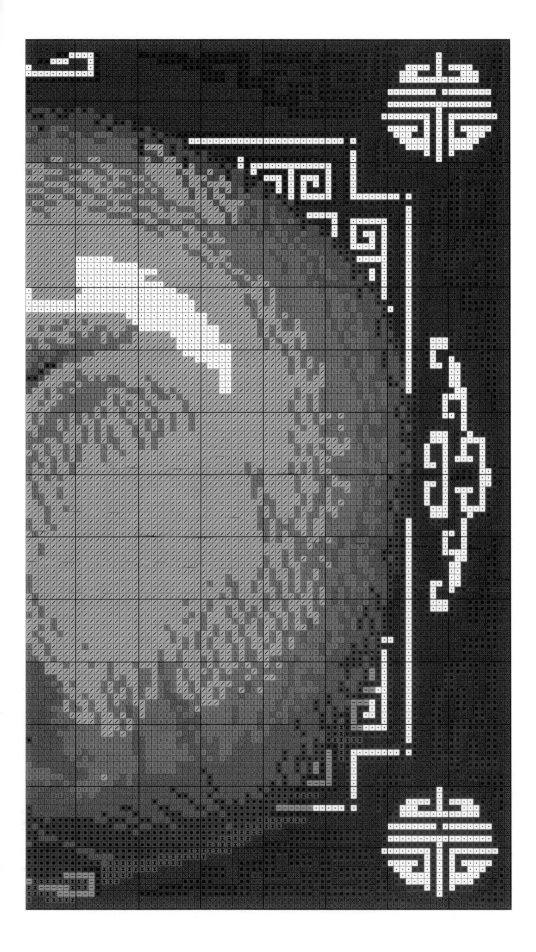

SIAMESE CUSHION

	DMC Tapestry Wool	No of skeins
■	Noir	5
•	Blanc	3
−	7618	1
✕	7666	5
✕	7110	1
‖	7949	4
U	7432	4
╱	7543	5
●	7469	3
S	7846	1
T	7713	1

PERSIAN CUSHION

	DMC Tapestry Wool	No of skeins
■	Noir	1
✕	7713	3
‖	7626	5
◣	7558	6
·	Blanc	5
✳	7139	1
≡	7640	3
✓	7603	1
✛	7600	1
T	7196	1
S	7951	1
Z	7949	1
◥	7973	1
╱	7433	2
○	7741	1
▲	7437	1
◪	7344	1
N	7341	2
★	7375	1
●	7228	3
∩	7257	1
I	7255	1
V	7219	1
L	7212	1

THE TURKISH ANGORA

Angoras are of Turkish origin and at one time all longhaired cats were known as Angoras because the earliest ones came from Angora (now Ankara). Although they were first taken to Western Europe in the sixteenth century, no clear distinction was made between them and Persians, and by the twentieth century they were scarcely seen outside Turkey. The true Angora breed was slowly becoming extinct as it was replaced by the Persian. However the breed was revived in the United States with white cats imported from the Ankara Zoo in 1962. It is now accepted in most of the colours and patterns.

The Angora has a long, sinuous body with a pointed head and large ears. The eyes are large and slightly almond-shaped, either blue or amber, or sometimes odd-eyed (one eye amber and one eye blue). The silky fur is fine, medium long, with a good ruff, full tail and tufts on the ears. It lacks the thick undercoat of the Persian cat, making it easier to groom. The Angora is a sweet-mannered cat, affectionate by nature and very intelligent.

THE BRITISH SHORTHAIR – MACKEREL TABBY

The British Shorthair is believed to have developed from the indigenous British cats. It is a solidly built, well-proportioned cat with a broad chest and short, strong legs on rounded paws. It has a massive, round head with full cheeks, set on a short, thick neck. The nose is straight and broad, the ears set wide apart and rounded at the tips. The expressive eyes are large and round. The coat is short and dense, and the tail short, thick and rounded at the tip.

The British Shorthair officially exists in seventeen separate colours, the Mackerel Tabby being one of these. The Mackerel Tabby differs from the Classic Tabby in that instead of blotches and butterfly shapes it has a single line running down the back, and from this a series of lines run vertically down the body. The tail is evenly ringed and lines feature on the neck, chest, face and head.

This cat is a strong, healthy and intelligent breed with skilful hunting abilities.

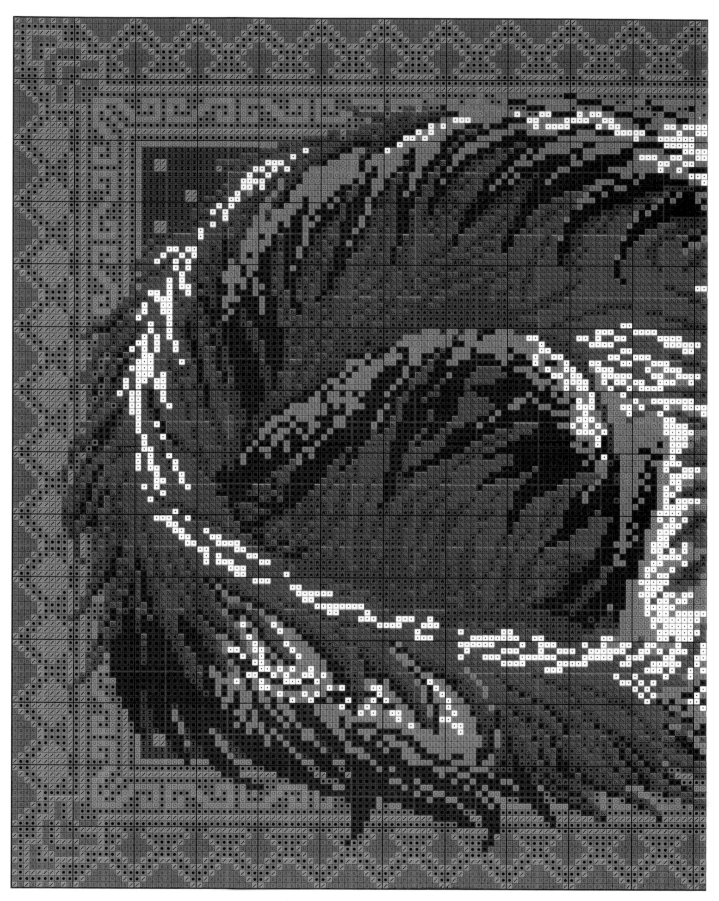

TURKISH ANGORA CUSHION

	DMC Tapestry Wool	No of skeins
■	Noir	5
✕	7626	1
○	7618	2
S	7592	2
★	7459	3
=	7518	1
⊳	7446	1
✕	7796	1
●	7797	4
·	Blanc	2
◺	7919	5
╱	7505	3
‖	7479	2
T	7526	1

BRITISH TABBY CUSHION

DMC Tapestry Wool	No of skeins
Noir	4
7558	1
7626	1
7713	1
7725	2
7742	1
7741	1
7947	1
7761	1
Blanc	3
7173	2
7846	1
7457	6
7458	4
7527	5
7385	1
7583	1
7364	1
7320	2
7387	1

PURRFECT GREETINGS CARDS

*A*s most of us know, cats absolutely adore sitting on the window-sill watching the world go by. With this in mind we decided to create this set of miniature designs for greetings cards incorporating all the lovely aspects of different window styles and their pretty floral surrounds.

MATERIALS *(for one card)*

- 22 count single-thread petit point canvas 20.5 x 18cm (8 x 7in)
- DMC six-strand stranded cotton as shown on the chart
- Tapestry needle size 28
- Thin card 20.5 x 38cm (8 x 15in) in a colour to complement your design
- A scalpel or craft knife
- Double-sided adhesive tape

Finished size

7.5 x 10.5cm (3 x 4in)

---

1 Mount the canvas in a frame following the directions on page 10. Following the appropriate chart, stitch the design according to the stitching techniques on page 11. Complete the needlepoint embroidery centrally onto the canvas using the required number of strands. If your finished needlepoint requires stretching before being made up, see page 12.

2 Once the needlepoint is complete, trim away any excess canvas leaving a 1.25cm (½in) border of unworked canvas all around.

3 Using the thin card, lightly mark a line every 12.7cm (5in) along the long side, in effect dividing it into three equal sections (see Fig 1). Using the scalpel or craft knife, cut an aperture measuring 10cm (4in) deep x 7.5cm (3in) wide from the central section. With the back of the blade, gently score the fold lines previously marked.

4 Place the needlepoint embroidery face up on a clean, flat surface and stick the double-sided adhesive tape on to the unworked canvas surrounding the embroidery. Take your card and position the aperture centrally over your embroidery. Press down firmly all the way round the window. Turn your card over to the wrong side and place double-sided tape round all four edges of the left-hand section. Fold this over and press to the back of the embroidery. Your card is now complete.

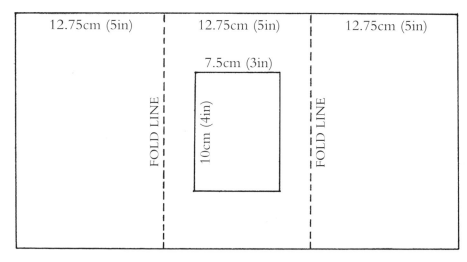

Fig 1

GREETINGS CARD

	DMC Stranded Cotton
■	310
⋈	318
○	415
·	Blanc
▲	601
U	603
=	605
◆	909
N	703
N	666
S	947
T	352
V	407
Z	3781
L	436
⁒	945
◣	307
✓	972
★	3820
I	470
×	799
●	798
+	333
−	794
✴	3371
I	869

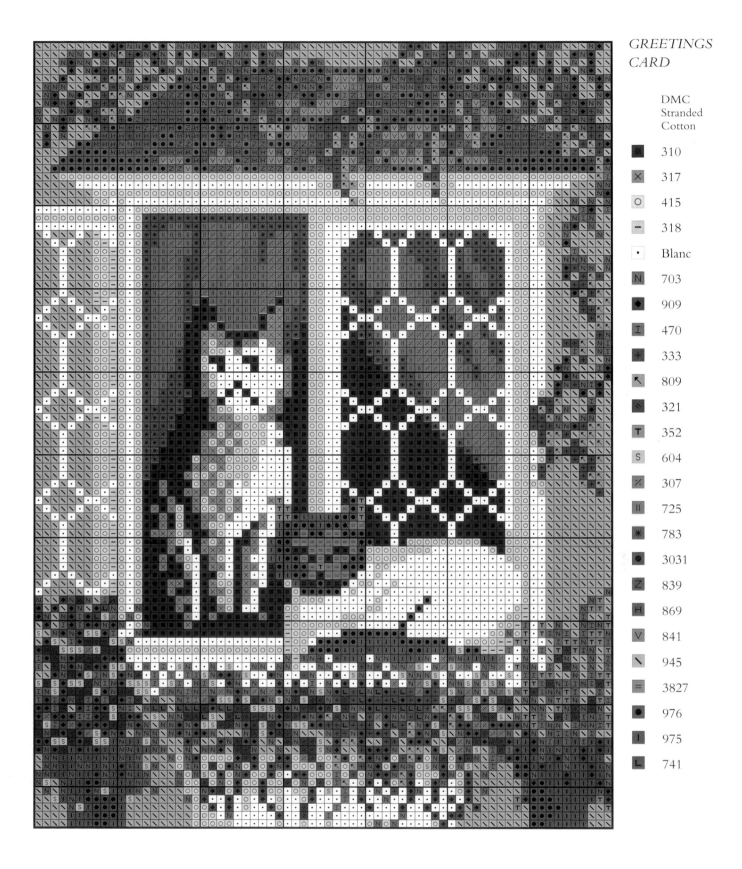

DMC
Stranded
Cotton

■	310
✕	317
○	415
−	318
•	Blanc
N	703
◆	909
I	470
+	333
K	809
◥	321
T	352
S	604
⁄	307
II	725
✳	783
◉	3031
Z	839
H	869
V	841
◣	945
=	3827
●	976
I	975
L	741

GREETINGS CARD

	DMC Stranded Cotton
■	310
▲	413
4	318
·	Blanc
⁒	437
◆	797
‖	799
\	800
✳	3371
T	801
Z	869
V	840
▽	352
S	301
–	402
O	3806
L	989
✕	987
●	909
N	333
→	307
÷	725
▢	740
+	793

GREETINGS
CARD

DMC
Stranded
Cotton

◆	3812
╱	959
L	964
■	310
Z	317
−	318
O	415
L	976
·	Blanc
✳	352
✕	436
≣	434
▲	898
S	3705
H	987
V	703
⬙	742
∩	740
∅	3806
→	307
+	3818
F	799
●	791
T	975

MOSAIC WALL HANGING

It is thought that domestic cats were introduced to Britain by the Romans but we do not know what these early cats looked like. Mosaics discovered at Pompeii and in Rome show brown striped tabbies, looking very much like the native wild cat of Britain and Europe. This can be differentiated from the domestic cat by its larger size, heavier build and by the blunt tip to its tail. The manner in which these cats are shown seems to indicate that the Romans regarded the cat as an exotic animal, ornamental rather than useful. One mosaic from Pompeii is said to be the finest representation of a cat to have survived anywhere in the ancient world. It was these beautiful historical pieces that gave us the inspiration for this design.

1 Mount the canvas in a frame following the directions on page 10. Following the chart on pages 84–5 stitch the design centrally onto the canvas, according to the stitching techniques on page 11. The design may require stretching after completion, if so, see page 12.

2 Once the needlepoint is complete, trim away any excess unworked canvas leaving 2.5cm (1in) of unworked canvas all round.

3 From your piece of fabric for the hanging straps cut six straps 12.7 x 23cm (5 x 9in). Stitch each

of these in turn, long edges together, right sides facing, with a 1.25cm (½in) seam allowance. Press the seam open, turn to the right side, placing the seam in the centre. Fold the straps in half lengthways, with the two short ends together and the seam on the inside, then pin and tack. Remove the pins.

4 Place your embroidery right side down on a firm, flat surface and pin the straps into position making sure that the sewing edge of the strap lies 1.25cm (½in) over the stitching line, while the loop lies to the centre. Position them evenly as shown in the photograph. Tack and machine stitch into place as close to the embroidery as you can.

MATERIALS

- 10 count double-thread canvas 37 x 49.5cm (14½ x 19½in)
- Backing fabric 34.5 x 47cm (13½ x 18½in) (of a similar weight to the finished needle-point)
- Matching fabric for the hanging straps 23 x 76cm (9 x 30in)
- DMC tapestry wool as shown on the chart
- Tapestry needle size 18

- Two 1.25cm (½in) diameter brass curtain rods 56cm (22in) long
- Four fancy brass curtain rod ends
- Gold cord 6mm (¼in) width x 91.5cm (36in) long
- Four gold tassels
- Matching sewing thread

Finished size

41 x 28.5cm (16 x 11¼in)

5 Place the backing material on the embroidery with right sides facing. (The hanging straps are sandwiched between the canvas and the backing fabric.) Pin and tack three sides together leaving a short side open, making sure you do not catch the straps in the seam.

6 Machine stitch around these three sides. Remove pins and tacking stitches. Turn to the right side so that the straps are released. Press in the seam allowance on the open edge, and slipstitch to close.

7 Place the brass curtain rods through the hanging straps and hang a tassel on each end before attaching the decorative ends. Stitch your cord into place round the curtain rod.

	DMC Tapestry Wool	No of skeins
■	7515	2
·	Blanc	6
‖	7445	3
╱	7171	6
✕	7165	1
✳	7318	2
U	7799	1
○	7952	1
Z	7513	2
▣	7861	1
▽	7314	1
●	7488	2
★	7995	1
L	7401	1

CAT SILHOUETTE FRAME

This 1920s-style design, with its stylized cats in silhouette, makes a lovely surround for a photograph of a loved one. It will make an attractive addition to your home, or be treasured if given as a gift to someone special.

MATERIALS

- 14 count single-thread canvas 29 x 26.5cm (11½ x 10½in)
- Firm mounting board 19 x 17cm (7½ x 6¾in)
- Thin card 19 x 17cm (7½ x 6¾in)
- White ribbon 6mm (¼in) width x 9cm (3½in) long
- DMC six-strand stranded cotton as shown on the chart
- Tapestry needle size 24
- Masking tape
- Scalpel or craft knife
- Craft adhesive or double-sided adhesive tape

Finished size

17.5 x 19cm (7 x 7½in)

1 Mount the canvas in a frame following the directions on page 10. Following the chart on page 88 stitch the design centrally onto the canvas, according to the stitching techniques on page 11 and using the required number of strands throughout (see page 8). You may find that your finished needlepoint will require stretching before mounting, if so see page 12.

2 Once your needlepoint is complete, trim away any excess canvas leaving 2cm (¾in) of unworked canvas all round the outside edge of the embroidery.

3 Using a sharp pair of scissors, make a small nick in the centre of the canvas, then cut diagonally from the centre up to each inside corner.

4 Take your mounting board and carefully cut out a central window measuring 11.5cm (4½in) deep x 9.5cm (3¾in) wide. Bear in mind that finished embroideries can vary slightly in size, so check your own inner frame measurement.

5 Place your embroidery face down on a firm, flat surface and position the mounting board centrally on top of it. Fold the triangles of canvas from the central window to the back of the board, trimming away any excess to fit, and secure them with masking tape. Next, fold in the outer edges of the canvas, mitring the corners (see page 13) and securing them with masking tape.

6 Using craft adhesive or double-sided adhesive tape, secure your photograph in position. Form the length of white ribbon into a loop and secure it to the back of the frame with masking tape, then fix the piece of thin card to the back of the frame with craft adhesive to create a neat finish.

CAT SILHOUETTE FRAME

DMC
Stranded
Cotton

- ■ 310
- · Blanc
- ✔ 726
- ‖ 827
- ✕ 209

SPECTACLE CASE

DMC
Stranded
Cotton

- ■ 310
- ● 414
- ○ 415
- · Blanc
- ✕ 976
- ‖ 434
- I 3773
- – 3772
- T 352
- Z 801
- ✳ 838
- S 869
- ⁒ 826
- ❊ 333
- + 726
- H 992

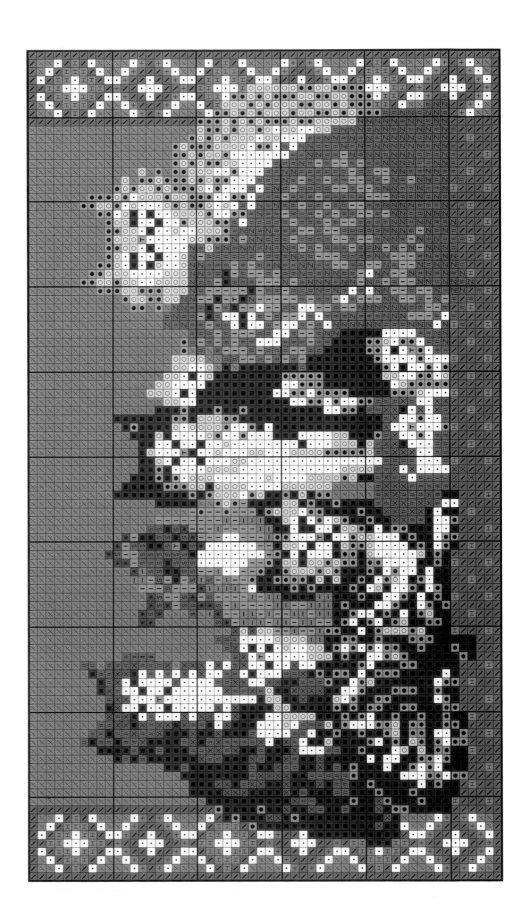

SPECTACLE
❧ CASE ❧

*T*his 'motley crew' of cats and kittens make a unique design
for a spectacle case for any cat lover. Whether you are
making this for yourself or as a gift for a special friend, it is
certain to become a treasured possession.

*The spectacle case (top right) is shown
here with the two wooden trinket
bowls, the tabby on the left and the
oriental shorthair on the right (see page
92 for instructions)*

MATERIALS
• 14 count mono canvas 16.5 x
24cm (6½ x 9½in)
• Backing fabric 12 x 19.5cm
(4¾ x 7¾in) (a similar weight
to the finished needlepoint)
• Two pieces of lining fabric,
such as cotton or calico, the
same size as the backing fabric
• DMC six-strand stranded
cotton as shown on the chart
• Tapestry needle size 24
• Matching sewing thread

Finished size
17 x 9cm (6¾ x 3½in)

1 Mount the canvas in a frame
following the directions on page
10. Following the chart on page 89
stitch the design centrally onto the
canvas using the required number
of strands (see page 8) and
according to the stitching techniques on page 11. If your finished
embroidery requires stretching
before mounting, see page 12.

2 Once your needlepoint is
complete, trim away any excess
canvas leaving a seam allowance of
1.25cm (½in) all round.

3 Place the embroidery and
backing fabric right sides together,
then pin, tack and stitch them
together along both long edges,
leaving the top and bottom open.
Trim across the corners, press the
seams open and turn through to
the right side. Take the two pieces
of lining fabric and stitch in the
same way. Press the seams open.

4 Place the backed embroidery
inside the lining right sides
together and stitch the tops
together. Turn through the opening
in the bottom of the lining and
slipstitch the opening together.
Push the lining inside the spectacle
case.

❦ WOODEN ❧
TRINKET BOWLS

*T*hese beautiful wooden trinket bowls are both useful and decorative. They can be used to adorn a dressing table, a small table or even a mantelpiece. A trinket bowl is an ideal present for any occasion or even just to say thank-you to someone special. The mahogany bowl features a British Shorthair Tabby while the elm bowl features an Oriental Shorthair.

MATERIALS *(for one bowl)*

- 18 count single-thread canvas 15cm (6in) square
- DMC six-strand stranded cotton as shown on the chart
- Tapestry needle size 26
- Heavyweight iron-on interfacing
- One round wooden trinket bowl with a 6.5cm (2½in) diameter lid
- All-purpose adhesive

Finished size

7.5cm (3in) diameter

1 Mount the canvas in a frame following the directions on page 10. Following the appropriate chart opposite, stitch the design centrally onto your piece of canvas using the required number of strands and according to the stitching techniques on page 11.

2 You may find that your finished needlepoint embroidery will require stretching, if so see page 12.

3 Iron the interfacing on to the wrong side of the work at this stage to prevent the canvas fraying.

4 Place the finished embroidery face up on a firm, flat surface and carefully disassemble the parts of the trinket box lid. Use the rim of the lid to centralise the design, then draw around the outer edge on to the canvas. Remove the lid and cut the canvas to this size.

5 To assemble the lid, replace the clear acetate and place your design centrally into the lid, with the right side towards the acetate. Place the sponge behind your design. Push the metal locking disc firmly into place, using thumb pressure, with the raised side of the disc facing the sponge.

6 When the locking disc is tightly in position, use a little all-purpose adhesive to secure the lid lining card to it. Finally, glue the felt disc supplied to the underside of the bowl.

Matching trinket bowls: the oriental shorthair (top) and shorthair tabby (bottom)

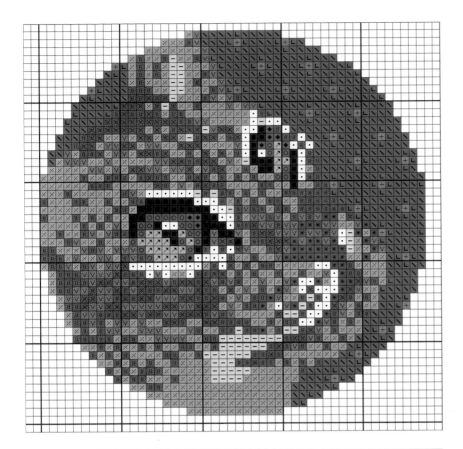

ORIENTAL SHORTHAIR

DMC
Stranded Cotton

■	310
·	Blanc
+	726
L	943
◆	312
O	322
↗	813
\	333
⁒	676
Ⅲ	680
✕	780
✳	3031
V	3829
−	677

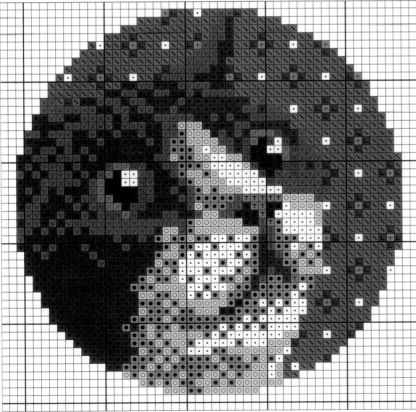

BRITISH SHORTHAIR TABBY

DMC
Stranded Cotton

■	310
●	414
O	415
·	Blanc
✳	3371
V	801
L	606
T	3778
S	3721
+	726
⁒	725
N	741
\	322

STAINED GLASS PICTURES

*W*alls were made for pictures, so what could be more appropriate than to display your handiwork — suitably framed — on your walls where it will be seen to advantage. Or give this delightful pair of pictures as a special and delightful present. These were inspired by the beautiful stained glass windows of the Art Nouveau period. Anyone who has a cat will know how much they love to sit on the window-sill watching the world go by, or just basking in the warmth of the sunlight streaming through the glass.

MATERIALS *(for one picture)*

- 10 count double-thread canvas 58 x 46.5cm (22¾ x 18¼in)
- Firm mounting board 47.5 x 36cm (18¾ x 14¼in)
- DMC tapestry wool as shown on the chart
- Tapestry needle size 18
- Masking tape
- Picture frame of your choice

Finished size

47.5 x 36cm (18¾ x 14¼in)

To stitch the right-hand picture of this elegant Art Nouveau pair, use the chart on pages 96–7, to work the other follow the chart on pages 98–9

1 Mount the canvas in a frame, following the directions on page 10. Following the appropriate chart, on pages 96–7 or 98–9, stitch the design centrally onto your piece of canvas, according to the stitching techniques on page 11.

2 As these designs are quite large, they may require stretching before being mounted for framing, if so see page 12.

3 To mount your needlepoint embroidery ready for framing, see page 12.

95

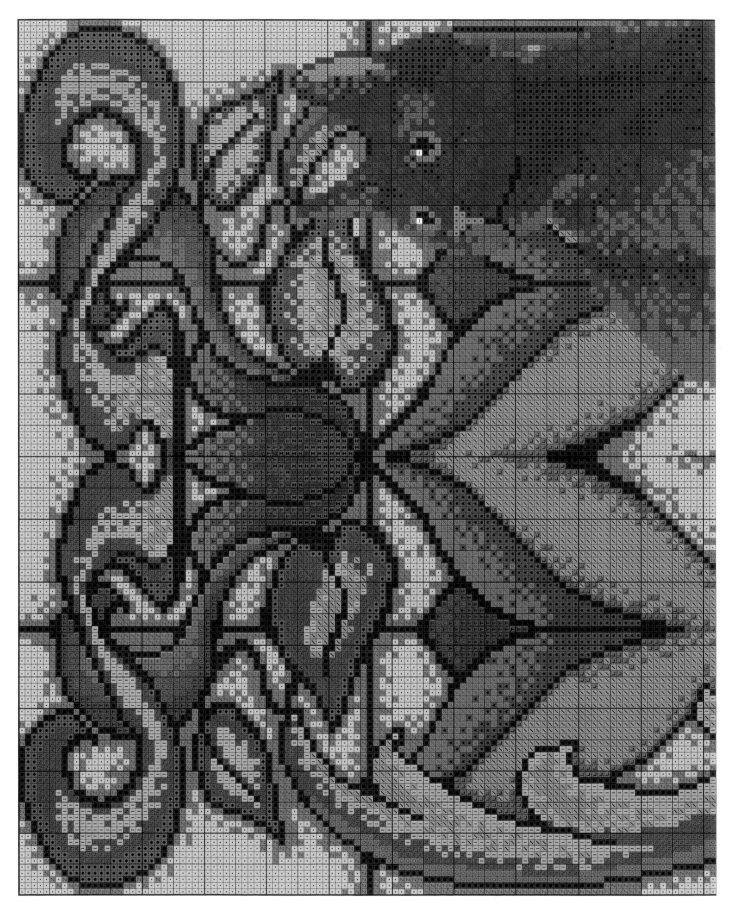

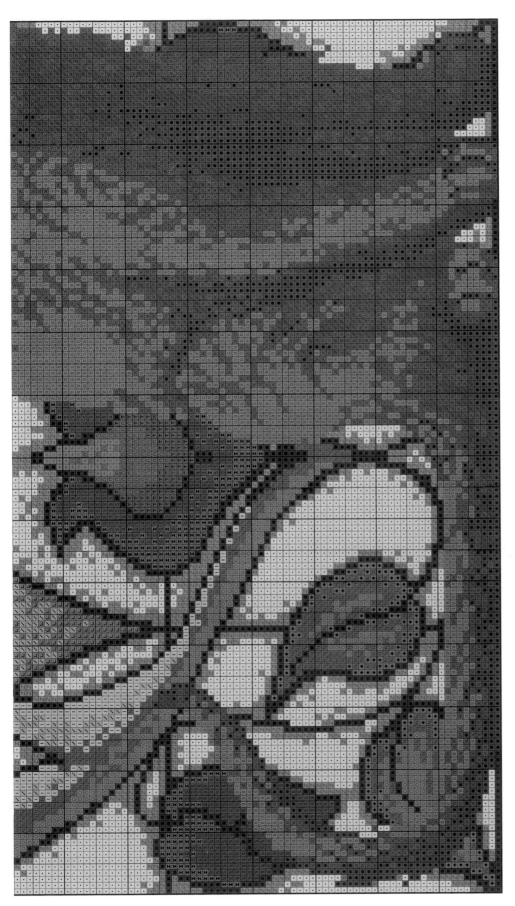

STAINED GLASS PICTURES

	DMC Tapestry Wool	No of skeins
■	Noir	4
✳	7618	1
✕	7110	1
S	7666	1
L	7364	1
╱	7584	2
÷	7433	1
∩	7436	1
T	7437	1
O	7909	1
◆	7348	1
⇒	7346	1
N	7915	2
I	7773	2
Z	7316	3
·	7799	4
★	7242	1
╱.	7255	1
●	7535	2
ø	7469	2
✕	7459	3
‖	7780	3
≡	7770	1
V	7519	1
–	Blanc	1

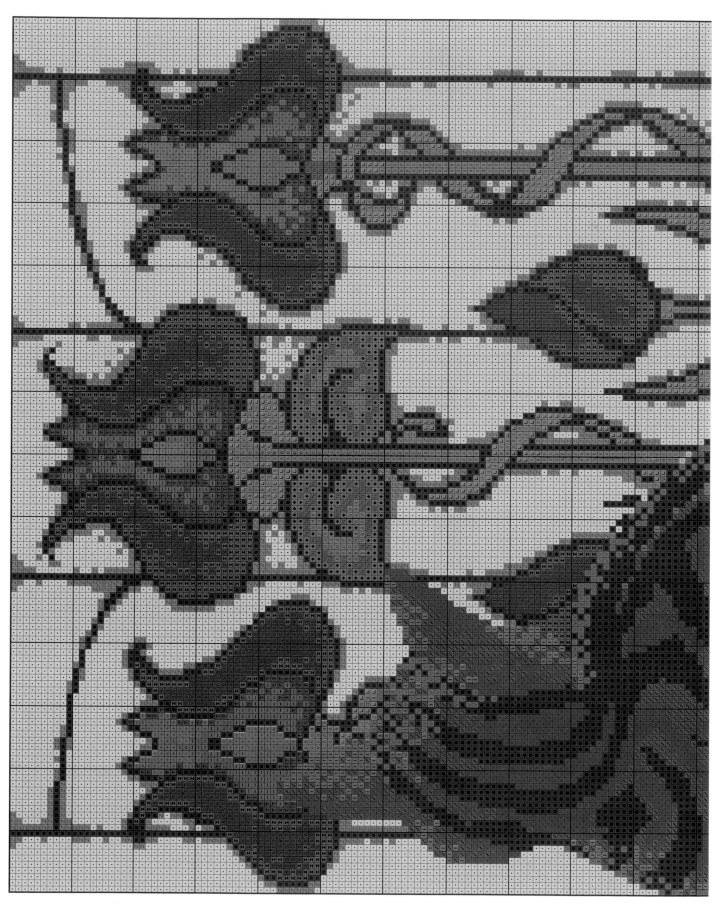

STAINED GLASS PICTURES

	DMC Tapestry Wool	No of skeins
■	Noir	7
V	7705	1
╱	7558	1
S	7666	2
X	7110	2
L	7768	1
‖	7341	2
T	7437	1
–	7973	1
÷	7433	1
◆	7348	1
N	7915	1
Z	7316	2
·	7799	9
I	7846	1
╱	7459	3
X	7469	3

BROWN TABBY SHAPED CUSHION

*T*his *delightful shaped cushion is intended to be fun as well as practical. It will create a lot of admiring glances perched on top of a bookcase, or sitting at the top of the stairs. Placed amongst a group of traditionally shaped cushions, the effect can be very pleasing. Although the chart shown is of a Brown Tabby, you can easily substitute your own colours to create your own unique cat. Simply transfer the outline of the cat onto a piece of graph paper, draw in the relevant details like the paws and face and then use coloured pencils to colour in the markings of your cat.*

1 Mount the canvas in a frame following the directions on page 10. Following the chart on pages 102–103, stitch the design centrally on the canvas, according to the stitching techniques on page 11. You may find that your needlepoint embroidery will require stretching before being made up, if so see page 12.

2 Once your needlepoint is complete, trim away the excess canvas leaving a 1.25cm (½in) border of unworked canvas all round.

3 Place the needlepoint onto the backing fabric right sides together, and pin into place. Cut out the backing fabric to the shape of the design (including the border of unworked canvas).

4 Make a tracing of the pattern for the base from the shape on this page and from the remaining backing fabric cut a piece for the base the same size.

5 Tack one half of the bottom of the needlepoint design onto the base. Then tack the design to the backing, leaving the other half of the base open and sew into place. Clip all inward shapes of canvas so that it will lay flat when turned to the right side. Turn to the right side and stuff firmly with kapok or polyester stuffing. Close the opening using slipstitch.

MATERIALS
- 10 count double-thread canvas 48.5 x 61cm (19 x 24in)
- Contrasting backing fabric 48.5 x 81cm (19 x 32in) of a similar weight to the finished needlepoint
- DMC tapestry wool as shown on the chart
- Tapestry needle size 18
- Matching sewing thread
- Kapok or washable polyester stuffing
- Tracing paper

Finished size
40 x 30cm (16 x 12in)

Use the template shown on this page to make the cushion base. Trace it off carefully then enlarge it by 160% on a photocopier

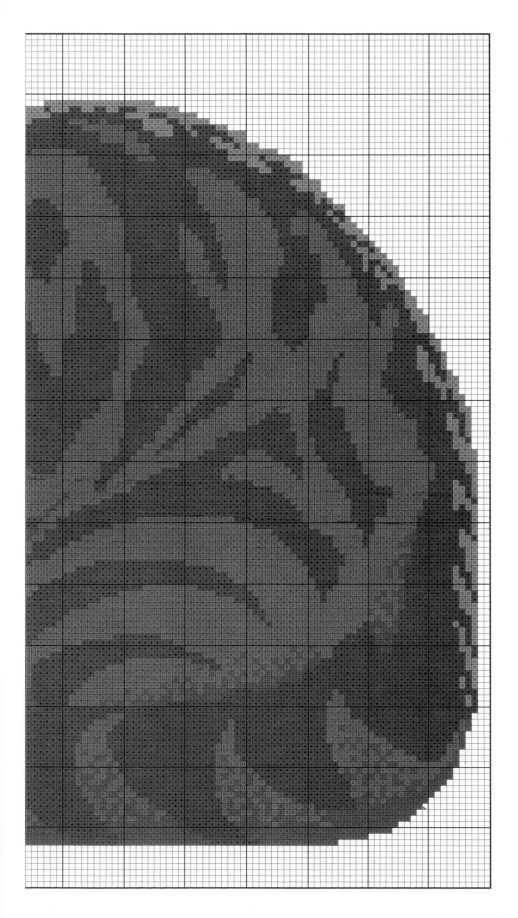

	DMC Tapestry Wool	No of skeins
■	Noir	1
·	Blanc	1
O	7558	1
≡	7341	1
T	7915	1
X	7620	1
‖	7466	9
╱	7179	1
S	7467	4
*	7533	8
▽	7850	1

COLLECTOR'S ❧CABINET❧

*T*his smart collector's cabinet is another unusual way of displaying embroidery. It is available from Framecraft Miniatures (see Suppliers page 127) and when painted blue is a perfect setting for this lovely design. Oriental Shorthair cats were the inspiration for this panel, where a pair of cats are shown gazing into the eastern sun.

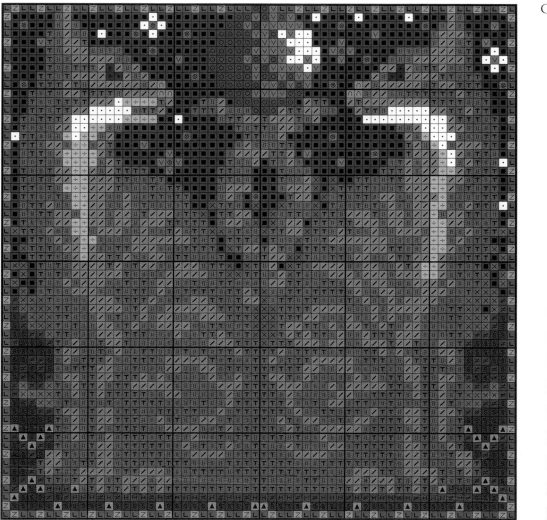

DMC
Stranded
Cotton

■	310
·	Blanc
◎	741
V	743
L	333
▲	989
Z	3821
■	820
X	996
S	321
H	815
⊗	703
⌀	721
T	801
‖	434
╱	436
÷	738
∩	352

MATERIALS

- 18 count single-thread canvas 18cm (7in) square
- DMC six-strand stranded cotton as shown on the chart
- Tapestry needle size 26
- Small collector's cabinet
- Masking tape
- Craft adhesive

Finished size

9.5cm (3¾in) square

1 Mount the canvas in a tapestry frame following the directions on page 10. Following the chart above stitch the design centrally onto the canvas using three strands throughout (see page 8) and according to the stitching techniques on page 11.

2 You may find that your finished needlepoint embroidery will require stretching before mounting, if so, see page 12.

3 Place the embroidery face down on a clean, flat surface and lay the grey mounting board provided with the collector's cabinet centrally on it. Fold the corners of the canvas over the board, mitring them to give a neat appearance (see page 13). Fold the remaining edges of the canvas over the board and secure them with masking tape.

4 Place the mounted embroidery in the cabinet recess, fixing it in place with craft adhesive.

BLUE LATTICE
❧PLACE MATS❧

*C*hinese lattice designs fill the backgrounds of this striking set of place mats. The cats featured are (clockwise from top left) Ming, Kiki, Rats and Thomas.

MATERIALS *(for each mat)*
- 10 count double-thread canvas 34 x 45.75cm (13½ x 18in)
- Calico for backing 29 x 40.5cm (11½ x 16in)
- DMC tapestry wool as shown on the chart
- Tapestry needle size 18
- Matching sewing thread
- Contrasting decorative edging 3mm (⅛in) wide x 1.25m (50in) long

Finished size
24 x 35.5cm (9½ x 14in)

---

1 First mount the canvas in a frame (see page 10). Following the appropriate chart, stitch the design centrally onto the canvas, according to the stitching techniques on page 11. Your embroidery may require stretching before being made up, if so, see page 12.

2 Trim the excess canvas leaving 2.5cm (1in) of unworked canvas all round the finished embroidery.

3 Lay the embroidery face up on a firm, flat surface and pin the decorative edging to the right side. Make sure that the sewing edge of the decorative edging lies just over the stitching line, while the decorative part when finished, lies to the centre. Tack into place.

4 Machine stitch the decorative edging to the canvas, stitching as close to the finished embroidery as possible. Remove all the tacking stitches.

5 Place the backing material on the canvas with right sides facing. (The decorative edging is sandwiched between the canvas and the backing fabric.) Pin and tack three sides together (two long sides and one short) making sure that you do not catch the decorative edging in the seams.

6 Machine stitch around these three sides then remove the pins and tacking stitches. Turn to the right side so that the edging is released. Press in the seam allowance on the open edge and slipstitch the open edge to close. Press on the wrong side.

MING PLACE MAT

DMC Tapestry Wool	No of skeins
Noir	1
Blanc	3
7796	3
7823	1
7798	2
7797	1
7705	1
7533	2
7467	2
7466	2
7174	2
7304	1
7302	1
7715	1

	DMC Tapestry Wool	No of skeins
■	Noir	1
·	Blanc	3
✗	7796	3
○	7798	2
✗	7624	3
‖	7293	2
╱	7558	2
V	7626	1
S	7547	1
↑	7549	1
✳	7840	1
T	7760	1
L	7122	1
∕.	7715	1
●	7797	1
◆	7823	1

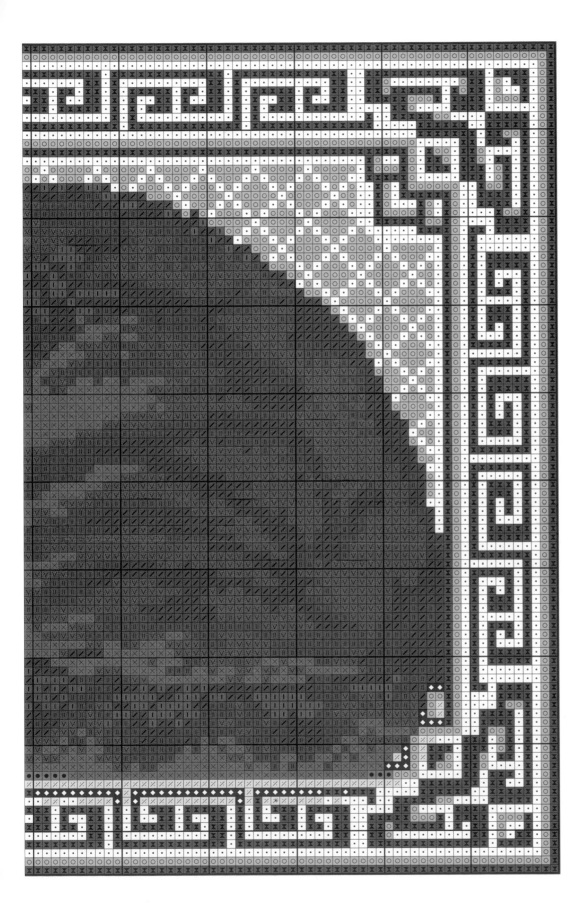

	DMC Tapestry Wool	No of skeins
■	Noir	1
·	Blanc	3
⁒	7715	1
✕	7796	3
◆	7823	1
○	7798	2
●	7797	1
I	7784	1
✕	7801	2
V	7401	2
╱	7922	2
II	7445	2
✳	7713	1
S	7626	1
→	7618	1
T	7124	1
I	7175	1

KIKI PLACE MAT

	DMC Tapestry Wool	No of skeins
■	Noir	3
·	Blanc	4
✕	7796	3
○	7798	2
✕	7705	1
∷	7617	1
Ⅲ	7488	1
╱	7780	1
▲	7850	1
<	7786	1
⊥	7784	1
✳	7515	1
╱	7715	1
◆	7823	1
●	7797	1

CAT IN THE MIRROR

*A*n unusual way of displaying needlepoint embroidery is in this useful mirror
(see Suppliers page 127). The design features an Oriental Shorthair cat with
an Indonesian inspired floral background.

MATERIALS

- 14 count single-thread canvas 23 x 19cm (9 x 7½in)
- DMC six-strand stranded cotton as shown on the chart
- Tapestry needle size 24
- One small, narrow Framecraft mirror
- Masking tape
- Double-sided adhesive tape

Finished size

9 x 12.5cm (3½ x 5in)

1 Mount the canvas in a frame following the directions on page 10. Following the chart stitch the design according to the stitching techniques on page 11, completing your needlepoint centrally onto the canvas and using the required number of strands (see page 8).

2 You may find that your finished embroidery will require stretching before mounting, if so see page 12.

3 Carefully disassemble the mirror recess. Place the needlepoint embroidery face down on a clean, flat surface and lay the grey mounting board (provided with the mirror) centrally on it. Fold the corners of the canvas over the board, mitring them to give a neat appearance (see page 13). Fold the remaining edges of the canvas over the board and secure them with masking tape

4 Clean the glass and place it in the mirror recess. Place your mounted embroidery face down on the glass, with the hardboard backing on top. With a screwdriver push the press points around the frame to hold the backing in.

5 Using double-sided adhesive tape, cover the back of the mirror with brown paper and then attach the hanger according to the manufacturer's instructions.

DMC Stranded Cotton

–	318	✳	915
>	415	O	3608
·	Blanc	●	3031
+	307	✕	898
S	741	L	434
▲	740	‖	841
■	924	╱	3774
Z	3812	T	760
V	964		

✤ZOE'S✤
FAVOURITE TOY

The needlepoint design on this footstool shows Zoe, a beautiful, sleek, black and white short-haired cat who shared many years of my life. She was a very playful cat who loved chasing and hunting. If the weather was inclement, she would continue her hunting prowess indoors on inanimate objects, sending them flying into the air with a deft swipe of her paw, bringing them down again with great expertise! She had many toys to 'hunt' but usually preferred to wreak havoc on the household! One toy she had a great love for was a little pink clockwork mouse which gave her (and me) many hours of enjoyment.

MATERIALS

• 10 count double-thread canvas 58.5 x 46.5cm (23 x 18¼in)
• DMC tapestry wool as shown on the chart
• Tapestry needle size 18
• Self-cover footstool (see Suppliers page 127)
• 6mm (¼in) rust-proof tacks or a staple gun
• Calico 48.5 x 36cm (19 x 14¼in) (optional)

Finished size
47.5 x 35cm (18¾ x 13¾in)

1 Mount the canvas in a frame following the directions on page 10. Following the chart on pages 120–121, stitch the design centrally on the canvas, according to the stitching techniques on page 11 and using the required number of strands throughout. As this design is quite large it may require stretching after completion, if so, see page 12.

2 Once your needlepoint is complete, trim it, leaving a 5cm (2in) border of unworked canvas all round the needlepoint.

3 To cover the footstool, first remove the top of the stool by undoing the screws, which are recessed under the frame. Put the screws in a safe place while you work. Lay your finished needlepoint embroidery right side down on a flat surface and place the footstool pad, face down, in the centre of your work, so that there is an equal amount of canvas showing on all sides.

4 Press the pad down on to the canvas along one of the long edges.

You may have to kneel on it if you are working alone or ask a friend to help you. Bring the canvas over the edge and secure it in place with the rust-proof tacks. Keep the canvas straight as you work, placing the tacks in the centre, then evenly spaced out to each end approximately 2.5cm (1in) apart. Alternatively, use a staple gun to hold the canvas in place. Repeat the process along the other long edge, pulling the canvas tightly and evenly into place.

5 Squeeze the pad down over the first short edge and fasten it in place as before. Mitre the folds of canvas in the corners to give a neat appearance on the right side (see page 13). Repeat the process on the other short edge.

6 If you wish, glue or sew a piece of calico or similar material under the pad to cover the tacked edges and give a neat appearance.

7 Replace the top of the stool, gently pressing it in the corners where the fit will be tight. Rescrew the top to the frame.

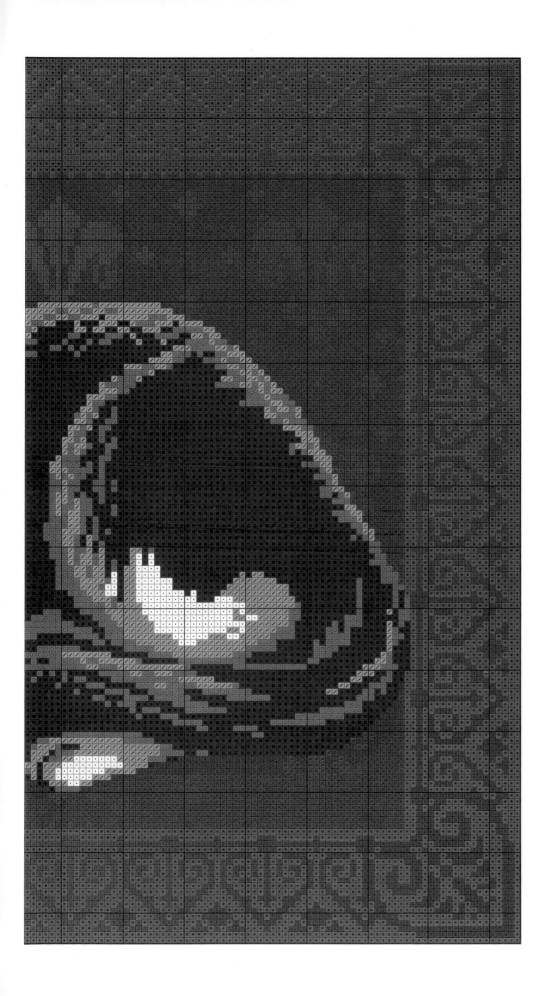

	DMC Tapestry Wool	No of skeins
■	Noir	4
·	Blanc	2
✳	7797	6
▯	7785	6
✕	7147	5
○	7626	3
╱	7617	3
▼	7915	1
▬	7583	1
▼	7850	1
H	7110	1
≠	7782	1
S	7199	1
L	7105	1
U	7895	1
╱	7853	1
◆	7820	1

SILVER TABBY KEY HOLDER

*T*his cheeky little Silver Tabby has the key of the door round his neck. Make sure you don't lose your keys by making this useful key holder to hang them on.

MATERIALS

- 10 count double-thread canvas 45.5 x 40.5cm (18 x 16in)
- DMC tapestry wool as shown on the chart
- Tapestry needle size 18
- Firm mounting board 40.5 x 35cm (16 x 13¾in)
- Masking tape
- Picture frame of your choice
- Five 2.5cm (1in) square brass cup hooks
- A bradawl

Finished size

26.5 x 32.5cm (10½ x 13in)

1 Mount the canvas in a frame following the directions on page 10. Following the chart on page 124, stitch the design centrally onto the canvas, according to the stitching techniques on page 11.

2 You may find that the finished needlepoint embroidery requires stretching before being mounted for framing, if so, see page 12.

3 Once your needlepoint is complete, trim away any excess canvas, leaving 2.5cm (1in) of unworked canvas all round the embroidery.

4 To mount and frame your finished embroidery see page 12. After this, attach the cup hooks to the bottom of the frame by making a small hole with the bradawl and screwing them in gently by hand, remembering to space them evenly.

SILVER TABBY KEY HOLDER

	DMC Tapestry Wool	No of skeins		DMC Tapestry Wool	No of skeins		DMC Tapestry Wool	No of skeins		DMC Tapestry Wool	No of skeins
▦	Noir	2	S	N7217	1	I	7548	1	I	7896	1
●	7626	2	‖	7726	2	L	7956	1	★	Fil or foncé gold thread	1
○	7558	1	N	7431	1	✳	7596	1			
·	Blanc	2	✕	7767	1	◣	7257	6			
T	7194	1	▲	7769	1	╱	7255	2			

MYSTICAL CATS PICTURE

This pretty little picture depicts the mystical nature of cats by featuring the ever-popular sun and moon theme. The feline models in this design are Matti and Lola.

MATERIALS
- 14 count single-thread canvas 23cm (9in) square
- Firm mounting board 13cm (5in) square
- DMC six-strand stranded cotton as shown on the chart
- Tapestry needle size 24
- Masking tape
- Picture frame of your choice

Finished size
13cm (5in) square

1 Mount the canvas in a frame, following the directions on page 10. Following the chart, on page 126, stitch the design centrally onto the canvas, using the required number of strands throughout (see page 8) and according to the stitching techniques on page 11.

2 If the finished embroidery requires stretching before being mounted for framing, see page 12.

3 To mount your embroidery ready for framing, see page 12.

MYSTICAL CATS PICTURE

DMC Stranded Cotton	DMC Stranded Cotton	DMC Stranded Cotton	
◼ 310	◣ 327	⋈ 3031	◫ 402
⬤ 317	◺ 725	✕ 801	◺ 783
◎ 318	N 471	T 352	▦ 304
⋅ Blanc	⫽ 799	‖ 435	— 433
			∗ 797

SUPPLIERS

DMC CREATIVE WORLD LTD
Pullman Road
Wigston
Leicestershire LE8 2DY
(For fabrics, threads, tapestry frames, scissors and needles.)

FRAMECRAFT MINIATURES
LTD
372-376 Summer Lane
Hockley
Birmingham B19 3QA
(For bell pull, collector's cabinet, miniature brass frames, wooden trinket bowls.)

MARKET SQUARE
(WARMINSTER) LTD
Wing Farm
Longbridge Deverill
Warminster
Wiltshire BA12 7DD
(For sewing box and footstool.)

COATS CRAFTS UK
McMullen Road
Darlington
Durham DL1 1YQ

Foreign suppliers and distributors of DMC and Framecraft products

FLEUR DE PARIS
5835 Washington Blvd.
Culver City
CA 90232
USA

GAY BOWLES SALES INC.
PO Box 1060
Janesville
W1 53547
USA

GREVILLE-PARKER
286 Queen Street
Masterton
New Zealand

IRELAND NEEDLECRAFT
Unit 4, 2-4 Keppel Drive
Hallam
Victoria 3803
Australia

I. C. KRAMER
2525 E. Burnside
Portland
OR 97214
USA

SERENDIPITY DESIGNS
11301 International Drive
Richmond
VA 23236
USA

WICHELT IMPORTS
RR #1, Hwy. 35
Stoddard
WI 54658
USA

GLOSSARY OF U.S. TERMS

The following list is for American readers who may not be familiar with some of the terms used in this book.

UK	USA	UK	USA
batting	wadding	oversew	overcast
cotton	floss	tacking	basting
cushion	pillow	wool	yarn

ACKNOWLEDGEMENTS

I would like to give a special thank you to all the ladies whose exceptional work effort in the sewing up of the embroideries for this book has been greatly appreciated. They have all worked extremely hard, and the high standard of their work is reflected in the beautiful finished pieces.

Thanks to: Jenny Whitlock, Louise Wells, Odette Coe, Maureen Hipgrave, Angela Taylor, Holly Jenkins, Diana Hewitt, Andrea Martin, Linda Guy, Jeanne Williams, Lynda Potter, Judy Riggans, Kit Shambrook, Constance Schofield, Josie Byrne, Helen Walker, Rita Boulton and Susan Grinstead.

Thanks also to two very important people who have been vital to the production of this book: my picture framer, Tom Aird; and my aunt Connie Woolcott, who has sewn up all of the finished embroideries into beautiful, functional pieces.